Eleanor,

with unforgettable memories and

with my love,

Helen

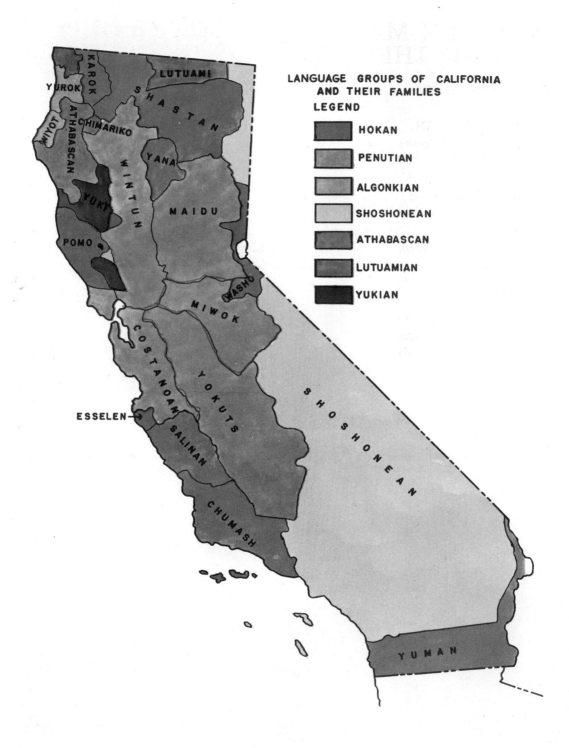

LANGUAGE GROUPS OF CALIFORNIA
AND THEIR FAMILIES

LEGEND

- HOKAN
- PENUTIAN
- ALGONKIAN
- SHOSHONEAN
- ATHABASCAN
- LUTUAMIAN
- YUKIAN

LUTUAMI

YUROK

KAROK

SHASTAN

ATHABASCAN

MIYOT

CHIMARIKO

YANA

WINTUN

YUKI

MAIDU

POMO

WASHU

MIWOK

COSTANOAN

ESSELEN→

YOKUTS

SALINAN

SHOSHONEAN

CHUMASH

YUMAN

SEVEN MAIN LANGUAGE GROUPS AND THEIR FAMILIES OR TRIBES

1. **ATHABASCAN:** Tolowa, Hupa, Chilula, Whilkut, Mattole, Nongatl, Sinkyone, Lassik, Kato, Wailaki

2. **ALGONKIAN:** Yurok, Wiyot
   (North)

3. **YUKIAN:** Huchnom, Coast Yuki, Yuki, Wappo
   (North)

4. **LUTUAMIAN:** Modoc
   (North)

5. **HOKAN:** Achomawi, Atsugewi, Yana, Yahi,
   (North Chimariko, Shastan, Yuma, Washo,
   and Esselen, Salinan, Chumash, Pomo, Digueño, Mohave
   Central)

6. **PENUTIAN:** Wintun, Maidu, Yokuts, Miwok, Costonoans
   (South
   and
   Central)

7. **SHOSHONEAN:** Paiute, Mono, Kawaiisu, Western Shoshonean (Panamint or Koso), Chemehuevi (or South Paiute), Tubatulabal, Serrano, Gabrielino, Cupeño, Juaneño, Luiseño, Cahuilla

See also: Maps of Tribes, pages 151, 152, 153, and Addenda: Chart of Tribes, Locations and Main Differences, pages 162–183.

California
Indian Days

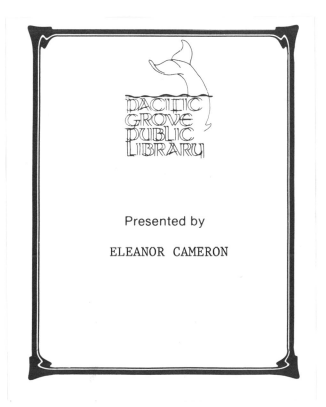

by Helen Bauer

CALIFORNIA INDIAN DAYS
CALIFORNIA MISSION DAYS
CALIFORNIA RANCHO DAYS
CALIFORNIA GOLD DAYS
HAWAII, THE ALOHA STATE
WATER: RICHES OR RUIN
JAPANESE FESTIVALS
THE AVOCADO COOKBOOK

Children's Press

California Indian Days

REVISED EDITION

Helen Bauer

LINE DRAWINGS BY DON FREEMAN

DOUBLEDAY & COMPANY, INC.
GARDEN CITY, NEW YORK

TO
the Logermans,
Roberta Jean and Calvin
and
their children,
Lynn Ann and Gail Ellen

my daughter and my grandchildren all in Houston

Acknowledgments

The Author wishes to give respectful acknowledgment to all authoritative sources of material on the subject of California Indians. The books from which I have reaped the facts presented in my book have been many and I hereby express sincere gratitude and a sense of obligation for all such help.

There are many who have furnished the important pictorial material contained therein. To all of them I give due credit and genuine appreciation. Among them are: Arthur Barr, president, Arthur Barr Productions, Inc., for permission to use the photographs of Indian life and who has furnished me with photographs for my other three California books; Hubert A. Lowman, my good friend, whose photographs have been used in all of my books; Karl Obert (photographs furnished by the California Conservation Council, Santa Barbara); Robert C. Frampton Photos, Claremont (assisted by my son, Dr. Sherwin Carlquist, Professor of Botany, Claremont Graduate School, Claremont Colleges and Rancho Santa Ana Botanic Garden, Claremont); R. M. Ariss, Department of Anthropology, Los Angeles County Museum; Robert H. Lowie Museum of Anthropology, University of California, Berkeley; the Museum of Natural History of Santa Barbara for permission to allow Bosworth Lemere, Carpenteria, to take photographs of the exhibits in the museum; the U. S. Forest Service (San Francisco); California Div. of Forestry (San Francisco); Division of Mines, State of California (San Francisco) for the relief maps; and the U. S. Bureau of Reclamation (Sacramento). Especial appreciation is due to Dr. Paul D. Scherer, Associate Professor of Industrial Arts, University of California, Santa Barbara, for making possible the production of the maps in the book.

Praise, appreciation and a full measure of credit goes to Don Freeman of Santa Barbara, a well-known and skillful artist, who is responsible for the artwork at the beginning of each chapter. The collaboration with him in the coordination of text and artwork has been a rewarding experience. His wife, Lydia Freeman, deserves and is hereby given a generous share of gratitude for her painstaking and carefully executed artwork.

Respectful appreciation is hereby given to three noted scholars in the scientific fields of Archeology and Anthropology; to Dr. James Deetz, Professor of Anthropology, University of California, Santa Barbara, author of *Invitation to Archaeology* (Natural History Press, New York, 1967); to Mr. Campbell Grant, artist and well-known authority on Indian rock art, author of *The Rock Paintings of the Chumash* (University of California Press, Berkeley, 1965) and *Rock Art of the American Indian,* (Thomas Y. Crowell Company, New York, 1967), Trustee of the Santa Barbara Museum of Natural History, who is presently engaged in a nation-wide survey of Indian Art for the National Science Foundation (see end-sheets); and to Dr. Arthur Rozaire, Curator of Archeology, Los Angeles County Museum (formerly with Southwest Indian Museum, Los Angeles), a recognized authority on Indian culture. All of these scholars have given unstintingly of their time and effort in evaluating and analyzing all material contained in this book in order that there be no question as to its authenticity. My sincere thanks are also given to the staff of the American Historical Society, San Francisco, for their helpful suggestions.

I offer my heartfelt appreciation to my many understanding friends who remained my true and loyal friends during the time I was "out of circulation" during the writing of this book.

A genuine expression of gratitude is due and hereby given to the able members of the editorial staff of the publisher for their ever-present understanding, patience, and friendly guidance.

One may spend endless hours in concentrated effort, but must also rely on the assistance and encouragement of family members. In particular, I acknowledge the help, faith, and patience of my husband, Roy M. Bauer. A rightful and full measure of credit is given to my son, Dr. Sherwin Carlquist, the constant guide, critic, and motivator of my writing and whose efforts were particularly helpful in the planning and securing of written and pictorial material on the subject of plants used by the Indians of that early time.

Contents

MAPS

Preface

California's story really began many thousands of years ago. Before any other peoples lived here, Indians roamed the oak-studded valleys and foothills; built their huts upon the river banks; lived along the beautiful coast and on the barren deserts. It is believed that there were about one hundred fifty thousand of them, more than in any other part of North America. They took food from the places they lived, as well as materials for their homes and all other things needed to meet the demands of their simple way of life. Not all the Indian groups were alike nor did they have the same skills and customs. The story of the California Indians must be general in scope. The material in this book covers the most constant features that were common to most tribal groups. However, there is a chart at the end of the book that attempts to outline some of the distinctive differences between the family groups.

The story of the California Indians is an interesting but sad one. Once they owned all of the land in California. You will want to read about the changes that came and what happened to these early-day Californians who began the first period in the history of California. Much of the period is only a dim memory. Place names, stone mortars and tools, painted rocks, stories told by early explorers and pioneers—these are all that remain as records of that time. We wish that we knew more about these people. As time goes on and places are found where Indians once lived, the story will be somewhat more complete. California Indians living today remember some of the history as told to them by their ancestors. But parts of it may only be imagined. It is hoped that those who read this book will gain an appreciation for and an understanding of the Indians who lived in California and knew it as their home.

California
Indian Days

Polar map showing close relation of Asia and North America. The people of Asia moved across the narrow strip of water and islands into North America.

Chapter 1

CALIFORNIA BEGINNINGS

Many moons ago in the faraway beginning years, California was a land of Indians. How and when they came to California no one really knows. There is no record to tell us; nothing was written, only remembered. Those who have studied about such things believe that the Indians came from Asia. They must have come to this continent long before there were boats that could cross an ocean. The only way they could have reached North America was through Alaska across the Bering Strait (see p. 17). At this point, Siberia and Alaska are about sixty miles apart. In between the two places are stepping-stone islands, the Diomedes. The longest distance between these islands is only about twenty-five miles. When the Bering Strait is frozen over, it can be crossed on the ice. The first people to come to this continent may have found a way over these icy areas. It is known also that this area was once dry land and they could have walked across from Siberia to Alaska. Whatever way they came or why they came is still a mystery.

The only facts known are that they came a long time ago and that the New World was settled by groups over a period of many years. Indians lived in central California about forty-five hundred years ago, and in the northwestern part, about two thousand years ago. Along the southern coast, the desert areas and west of the Sierra Nevada (Snowy Mountains), it is believed that Indians were in California about fifteen or more thousand years before white settlers came.

Scientists guess that the Indians went southward from Alaska to Canada. At that time Canada was also a land covered with ice and snow. For several thousand years there was an ice-free avenue in Canada and south of Canada along the Rocky Mountains. Some groups wandered to the east and still others went farther and farther south and some went to the southernmost tip of South America (see map).

Finds have been made proving that people lived in America at a time when large animals roamed the land. Among them were large camels, mammoths, giant sloths, and other (late) Ice Age animals. Changes in the weather, such as rain, snow, ice, and movements of water, drove animals onward. People also moved onward not only because of the weather, but because they needed animals and plants for food. They may not have wanted to move on but nature and the need for food pushed them along. They may not have known exactly where they were going except that they were following the animals and plants ahead of them.

No one knows just how many Indians settled in California. Some think that there were as many as 130,000 to 150,000 of

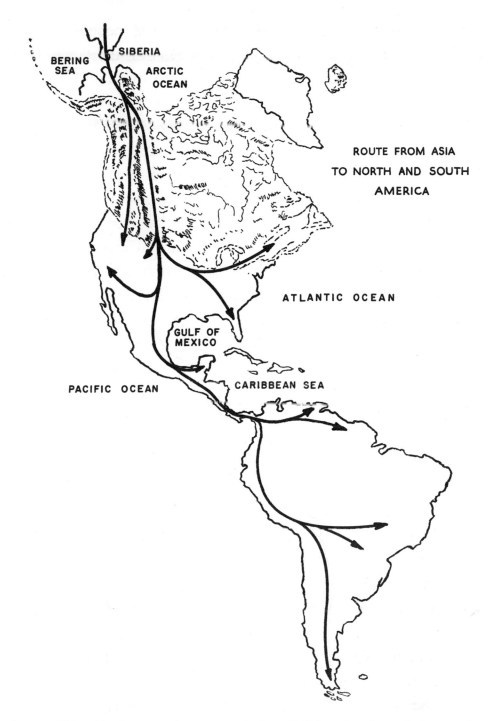

SIBERIA

BERING SEA

ARCTIC OCEAN

ROUTE FROM ASIA TO NORTH AND SOUTH AMERICA

ATLANTIC OCEAN

GULF OF MEXICO

PACIFIC OCEAN

CARIBBEAN SEA

them. The Indians who stayed in California found it to be a good land where they could build their simple homes, and where they could hunt and fish. The climate was warmer than in other places they had been and most important to them, there was an ample food supply. Wherever Indians settled in California, whether in the mountains, hills, valleys, or desert, they knew that the new land belonged to them and that it always would.

For thousands of years these people lived and worked with only tools they made of bone, stone, and shell. They had fire; they roasted meat and cooked other foods to meet their needs. There were no horses or cattle. Planting of crops, except along the Colorado River in the south, was not known. No one had to teach them to sew, cook, or build because from the earliest times they had known how to do these things. They lived with the world they found. There was a deep religious feeling for everything about them—the stars, trees, stones, mountain peaks, and streams.

In those early years when California was young, the Indians felt happy and free from danger. Then in 1542 came another people with pale skin, unlike their own. Perhaps the brown-skinned people wanted to say to them, "Go! Leave us in peace!" These strangers to California's shores were explorers sent by Spain. They were the first ones to record Indians living in California. Their records give us the earliest descriptions of the people and the life they lived at that time.

It was June of 1542 when Juan Rodríguez Cabrillo, a Portuguese explorer sent by Spain, sailed from Mexico. In those days maps were very poor but Cabrillo hoped to find a passage through or around unknown land (California was thought to be an island) that would prove to be a short way to India. He had been told, "Sail north along the western coast. See if the land is fertile and green along the shore. See if anyone is living there. Try to find good harbors."

At times the wind beat back the white-sailed *San Salvador* and the smaller ship, *La Victoria*. When there was no wind, the ships bobbed about like corks in the quiet sea. Cabrillo could

Indians knew that this beautiful new land belonged to them. (Harriet E. Huntington)

only wonder where the winds would carry them. For three months he headed northward. He watched carefully but saw no way through the land but one day he found an open place along the shore. He and his men guided the ships toward it and found it to be a "good and safe harbor" (present-day San Diego Bay). Even then Cabrillo did not know where he was.

The sailors could see dark-skinned people running about along the shore. When they landed they found only a few Indians who had not run away from the strangers. Cabrillo held out his hands with palms upward to show that he and his men wished to be friendly. After a few days some of the Indians came back. To them Cabrillo gave beads and small gifts. How very strange these men with white skins must have looked to the Indians! Perhaps they thought of them as gods from the "spirit world." The ships sailed on but, before he left, Cabrillo had given the name of San Miguel to the "safe harbor."

The weather was good and the wind right. The ships sailed northward again and anchored at an island we now know as Santa Catalina. Here the Indians were very friendly and made the strangers welcome. Leaving the island, Cabrillo kept close to the coast. He noted the pleasant country with its valleys, plains, and mountains. Coming close to the land, his men saw smoke from many fires. The ships anchored near the shore where many small villages could be seen. Cabrillo named the place the Bay of Smokes (*Bahia de los Fumos*). It is believed that this was present-day San Pedro Bay.

The two ships continued sailing along the coast. Near what is now called Ventura, canoes paddled by Indians darted out through the waves to meet the strange ships with white wings. Cabrillo thought a good name for this place would be the Town of Boats (*el Pueblo de Canoas*). The sailors visited the villages along the shore and the white men and the Indians

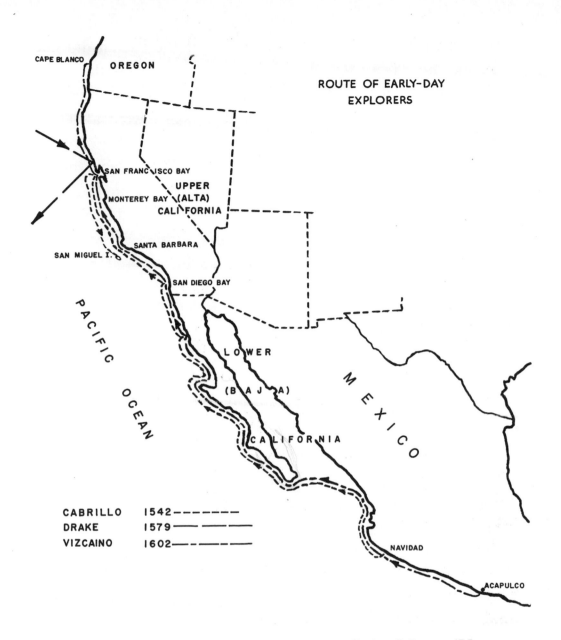

ROUTE OF EARLY-DAY
EXPLORERS

CAPE BLANCO

OREGON

SAN FRANCISCO BAY

UPPER
(ALTA)

MONTEREY BAY

CALIFORNIA

SANTA BARBARA

SAN MIGUEL I.

SAN DIEGO BAY

PACIFIC OCEAN

LOWER

(BAJA)

CALIFORNIA

MEXICO

NAVIDAD

ACAPULCO

CABRILLO   1542 --------
DRAKE   1579 —— —— ——
VIZCAINO   1602 --- --- ---

gave gifts to each other. At a point near Point Mugu (Ventura County), Cabrillo raised the flag of Spain, on October 10, 1542. From that day on, California was supposed to belong to Spain.

Records from that time show that Cabrillo's ships stopped at several places along the Santa Barbara coast. One place was Dos Pueblos (Two Towns) where there were two Indian villages (*rancherías,* the Spanish called them). Between the villages was a small stream. Indians on one side of the stream did not look like nor speak the same language as those on the other side. Those in one village were short and fat and those in the other were thin and taller and their skins were a lighter color.

Heavy winds forced the ships out to sea. They found shelter in a snug harbor on San Miguel, one of the Santa Barbara Islands. Here again the explorers were received with kindness. On this island Cabrillo fell and broke his arm. However, he had no thought of turning back and so he ordered his men to sail on toward the north. They ran into storms and rough seas and there was no land in sight. Then Cabrillo saw a curve of land like a bay (Monterey Bay). It looked like a good harbor but he could not find out because of the stormy weather. There seemed to be nothing to do but turn back to the island near the Santa Barbara coast. All this time Cabrillo's arm had been getting worse. He fell ill and died while his ships were in the island harbor. The sailors buried the brave Cabrillo on the island of San Miguel. Before he died Cabrillo had told his pilot, Bartolomé Ferrelo, "Go on and on. Do what I was not able to do." Ferrelo and his men sailed as far north as Oregon. No way was found through the land. No "cities of gold," as the old stories reported, were found by the men. So the ships turned homeward again. Cabrillo and his men had not discovered a short cut to India but they did find out many things not known before about that part of the world. Their journey had taken them all the way up the coast of South America and eight hundred miles up the Pacific Coast. Now they knew that there was a mainland, not just one large island or a group of small islands through which ships could pass. They brought back news about the beautiful land they had seen and about the friendly Indians living there.

For almost fifty years after Cabrillo's voyage, other explorers came from countries in the Old World. Their records also tell about the Indians living in California. The last explorer who came during those early years was Sebastián Vizcaíno, in 1602. Then, strange as it seems, California was forgotten for more than a hundred and sixty years. The Indians lived on as they had always done before the explorers came. Nothing really changed at all.

An Indian village in those days must have been a lively place. People were working, chatting, hunting, dancing, playing, singing. Today these villages with their busy, happy people are all gone.

How do we know what they were like, what kinds of foods and homes they had and the many things that were used in their daily lives? Aside from the records of explorers, the early-day Indians left us their record, not one told in words but in stone and bone. When there are no written records, scientists (called archaeologists) try to find out what life was like in the early years. They hunt and dig until they find objects left from the distant past. They try to describe and explain what they find. The age of the material found gives a clue as to when it was used. The deeper the objects are buried, the older they are. Then the scientist tries to explain what these objects are, their probable use, what materials were used and how they were made. It is in this way that some kind of idea is formed as to where, when, and how people once lived.

The early-day Indians left their secrets in caves, shell mounds, ashes and in graves buried deep in the earth. The California Indians left behind no famous ruins of cities, no temples or great works of art as some other people (such as the Mayans of Mexico) had done. What they left were things that told of their simple but useful way of living—tools of chipped stone, spearheads, arrow points, grinding stones; seeds, animal bones, bits of baskets or pottery. Where a number of arrow points, spear points and animal bones were found buried, it is probable that the area was once a hunting camp. Where holes worn in rock are found, women must have spent hours, grinding acorns because these rocks are found where many oak trees grow. So everything that is found tells a part of the story of that time.

Early Californians who lived along the coast ate clams, mussels, and other seafood and threw the shells into heaps by the sides of their villages. The piles of shells grew from heaps into great mounds. In the San Francisco Bay area alone, over four hundred such mounds have been found and once there were probably more. Shell mounds have been found along the shore in Santa Barbara and on the Santa Barbara Islands. Wind and rain have beaten against the mounds but the broken shells have held together during the years and have given us a clue as to where villages once stood.

Many thousands of Indian objects have been found in California during the last hundred years. Many of them have been found by accident and have been kept by the finders. However, others are in museums where visitors may see them. Scientists spend their lives in search of these objects. Every year more and more of them are found. In this way, bit by bit, pieces of the puzzle can be put together to help us understand something of the life of that time. By this kind of careful study, scientists are gradually reaching further and further back into the past, and proving that Indians were in California thousands of years ago.

Besides the records of early explorers and the Indian objects that have been found, we have still another clue as to the people and customs of that long-ago time. From the cradle to old age, Indians learned the history of their people. There are Indians still living in California who remember stories of early days told to them by their parents and grandparents. These stories had been passed on from age to age and tribe to tribe,

Indians left their secrets buried deep in the earth. (*Exhibit, Santa Barbara Museum of Natural History, Bosworth Lemere*)

through many hundreds of years. As time goes on and more studies are made and more objects are found, it is hoped that we will know even more than we do now about those early Indian days. We are fortunate to know as much as we do about these first Californians.

Chapter 2

TRIBES AND VILLAGES

Even though there were many thousands of Indians in California, the state is so large that they could not have lived in all parts of it. Wherever they lived, however, they must have loved their beautiful California home. There were towering mountains, some snow-covered most of the year. High-set valleys had great stony cliffs around them. Lower valleys were green or sometimes brown, and in spring there were wide carpets of blue, purple, and gold-colored flowers. There were fish in the rushing rivers and quiet lakes, and wild animals in the forests. Trees and bushes were heavy with acorns, seeds, nuts, fruits, and berries. West of the mountains was a very long shore-

There were towering mountains, some snow-covered most of the year. (Harriet E. Huntington)

Wild animals were in the forest. (Karl Obert)

line. Here waves lapped and foamed against rocks or rolled up on the sandy beaches.

Early-day California Indians who banded together and lived in certain territories thought of themselves as people of a village or a family group related to each other. A family group or community had a main village with smaller villages (sometimes known as "tribelets"). Even though the family group lived in several settlements in a given territory, they acted as one related group. The very large tribes who lived in other parts of America did not exist in California.

So far as we know, there were more languages spoken by the California Indians than by any other group in the United States. At one time there were twenty-one separate language groups

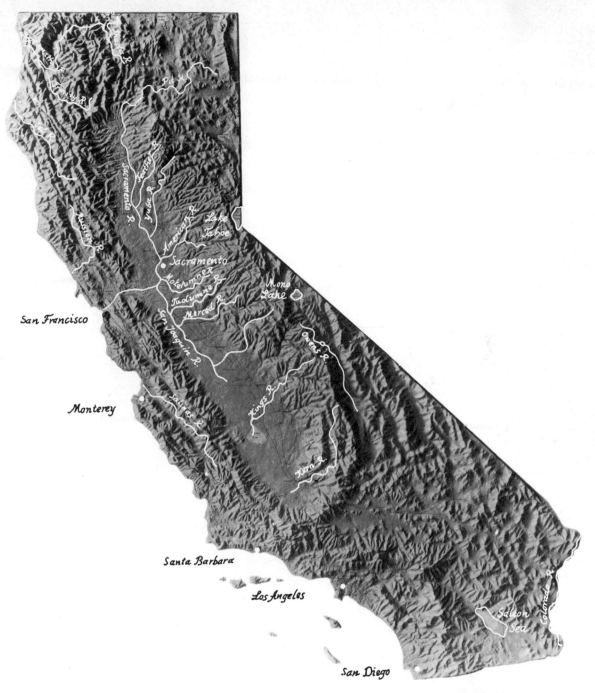

Indians lived along the seacoast, by lakes, along main rivers and their branches.

with seven main divisions. Within the seven language groups there were fifty small divisions (or small tribes) and a great number of independent villages. It was possible that those within a family language group did not understand each other as there

They lived in the valleys. (*Harriet E. Huntington*)

were 135 dialects or ways of speaking the same language. Even then many of their words had different shades of meaning.

Wherever a village was located, a water supply had to be nearby. Usually the larger villages were near the larger streams. Some villages were along the coast where there was a fresh water supply. Some were on flat lands in valleys that were near rivers or springs. On the desert, villages were built near water holes.

These were their more permanent homes but groups did leave their homes in different seasons to gather various foods as they ripened. There must have been much moving about as the seasons changed—from the valleys to the hills and from the hills to the valleys. Usually the headman of the village was the leader and led his people to the food-gathering places each season.

Some of the villages had only a few families; some had hundreds. The Chumash villages, for example, were many and scattered along the coast from the Los Angeles area to San Luis Obispo and on the Santa Barbara Channel Islands. Around Goleta there were twenty-five to thirty villages. An explorer's journal said that there were about one hundred houses and a thousand people living near Santa Barbara (near the entrance to present-day University of California, Santa Barbara). Dos Pueblos (on the Santa Barbara coast) with its two villages had about a thousand people. It was reported that there was a cluster of five other Chumash villages in which there were several thousand Indians living.

The Yokuts of San Joaquin Valley had a larger tribe or family group (about twenty thousand) and spoke a language unlike any other. The Yokuts were thought to be more like a true tribe as known in other parts of the United States. Their villages were small but there were many of them. Even though there were more Yokuts, the Shoshoneans had the largest territory in California. (See color map in front of book.)

Chapter 3

WHAT WERE THESE

INDIANS LIKE?

The Indians varied in their looks from tribe to tribe just as they did in their customs and languages.* Some of them were short and of heavy build. Some had narrow heads with thin faces and were tall. People of the Yuki tribe were short and had narrow heads and broad noses. The Mohaves in the south had broad heads but were a tall people.

In some of the tribes the Indians had dark brown skins. These were the ones who lived near the ocean or in warmer places. Other Indians had skin no darker than a light tan. It is known that all of them had dark brown eyes.

All of the Indians had straight black hair. Almost all of them

* See Addenda: "Tribes, Locations, and Main Differences."

wore their hair long. Some of the men tied it up at the back of their neck and stuck a hunting knife in the knot. What a handy place for that when they went hunting! Chumash women wore their hair cut in bangs across the front. They took great pride in the long hair that hung over their shoulders. Sometimes they wore bands of shells around their heads like flat crowns. Thin, bone hairpins have been found and so we know that some women used them. Hair was brushed with a little bundle of stiff fibers. Some of the women mixed mesquite gum with clay and left it on their hair for a few days. When washed, the hair was clean and shiny. Young women and girls may have tucked flowers into their hair.

Some have thought that California Indians lived in a very poor way, worked very little, and had few arts and crafts. Those who have studied about them have found that this is not true. Some of the groups had great skill in making baskets. Not much pottery was made, but what was, was designed rather well. The Chumash men built wooden canoes that were much different from any others built by Indian tribes in North and South Amer-

Fiber hairbrush.

Women wore ornaments even when they went food-gathering. (*Los Angeles County Museum*)

It is surprising to learn that these early-day people made objects so well (steatite bowl, steatite boat-shaped charm, steatite whale charm, bone harpoon point, bone fishhook, stone knife). (Southwest Museum, Los Angeles)

ica. They were the only ones made of planks of wood sewn together with leather strips and sealed with tar. Beautiful ornaments were made by coastal Indians and traded to inland tribes. Bowls, pipes, and other soapstone (steatite) articles were of good design and polish. Some were inlaid with bits of shiny shells. Other articles that proved their skills were the mortars, pestles, arrow points, and all kinds of useful things made by patient work. It is surprising to learn that these early-day people made as many objects as they did with no modern metal tools to help them.

White settlers who came to California sometimes called the

Exhibit shows use of mortar and pestle, metate and mano, and cooking with hot stones. (Santa Barbara Museum of Natural History, Bosworth Lemere)

Indians "Digger" Indians. They saw women digging in the earth day after day. Their main responsibility was to gather food and sometimes the food was underground. Women used digging sticks to dig up roots and bulbs that were used for food. They dug for roots used in making their baskets and they helped dig out the ground for their homes. So, it is true that they did dig, but there was never a "Digger" tribe of Indians in California and no such name should ever be given to them.

Many think of Indians as being warriors. For hundreds of years most of the California Indians lived in peace with each other. When the explorers found them they were a happy, contented people most of the time. They were slow to anger, and only waged war when they had been wronged. At that time their only enemies were other Indian tribes that came into their territory to take food. Each tribe had its own area or territory and no member of another tribe or family was allowed to take food from another unless told that he could do so. If a tribe had more food than could be used by its members, it was glad to trade with those of other tribes. It was only when white settlers took away their land that Indians really fought back.

Southern California Indian woman making acorn meal. (Exhibit, Los Angeles County Museum)

Chapter 4

DEERSKINS AND NECKLACES

In those far-off early years, clothing worn by the Indians was very simple and varied with the climate and season. If hot, they wore less; if cold, they wore more. Usually little clothing was worn and little needed. In the warm summer months the men wore nothing at all or just a skin or yucca fiber loincloth folded about their hips. What they lacked in clothing, they made up for in the decoration of their faces and bodies. This was done by painting red, black, and white designs in figures and stripes. White paint was supposed to fool the "evil spirits" and scare them away.

Paints could be washed off but not the tattoo designs, which were made by pricking the skin with cactus spines or something sharp. Dyes or black soot from the fire were rubbed into the

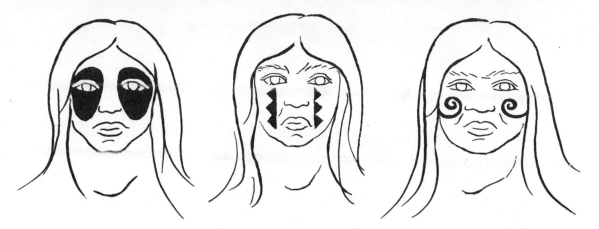

Mohave (Mojave) men—face paint designs.

designs pricked on the skin. Women liked tattoos even more than the men. They believed that the deep-blue dots and lines made them quite beautiful.

Women wore a short skirt in two pieces, the narrow, smaller one worn in the front. A larger but shorter piece came around the hips to meet the front skirt or apron. Skirts were made of deerskin or other animal skins or from fibers. The bottom half of a skin skirt was slit into strips or fringes. Such skirts made walking or sitting at work easy. Fiber skirts were made from the inner bark of trees or tule, shredded and gathered together on a fiber cord. Women liked to decorate the ends of the fringes with bits of tar, tiny shells, or even pine nuts. Some women dyed the skirts a bright red.

Men as well as women liked to wear ornaments. Men's necklaces were of birds' beaks, animal teeth, or large shells. Ear ornaments were rods about the size of a small finger, made of wood,

Mohave (Mojave) women—face paint designs.

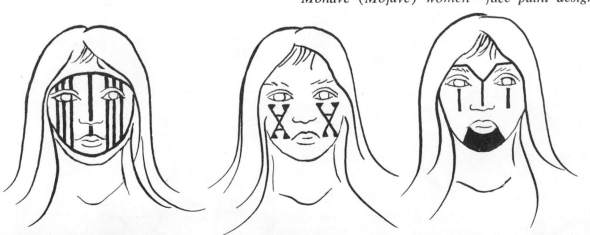

Fringed skirts made it easier to sit while working. (Arthur Barr Productions, Inc.)

Women wore caps to protect their foreheads when carrying burden baskets. (Santa Barbara Museum of Natural History, Bosworth Lemere).

bone, shell, or an animal's tooth. These were put through a hole in the ear.

Indian women were especially fond of ornaments and beads of all kinds. The favorite ones were strings of many-colored shells, or of bits of soapstone and bone. Beads with very fine carvings on them have been found. Some strings of beads were so long that they hung to the waist and many of them had ornaments on the ends. Strings of shells were worn around the wrists also. Hairbands and belts were made of brightly colored birds' feathers and bits of shells.

Indian women wore caps or hats not to protect them from the sun. For them, the pretty little tightly woven caps had another important use. This was to protect their foreheads when carrying heavy burden baskets in nets when they went out food-gathering. Some of the caps were coiled and some twined just like the baskets made in various areas. (See Chapter 9.) Usually the caps were made round to fit the head. The Shoshonean women wore peaked ones while the flatter-shaped caps were worn by most other tribes.

Young children wore no clothes at all. Older girls wore skirts

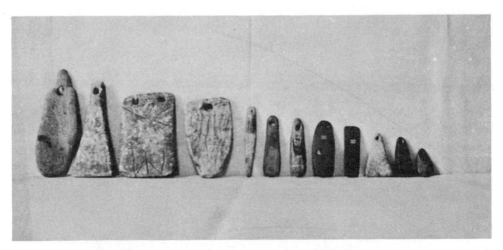

It is believed that most of these were pendants of various sizes and materials worn on necklaces. (Southwest Museum, Los Angeles)

like their mothers. Young boys wore the same kind of skins around their hips as their fathers did.

Moccasins of skin, tule, or yucca fiber were their shoes. It was pleasant to go barefooted around the village during the summer months. Moccasins were worn only on wood- or food-gathering trips or perhaps in cold weather. When the father took out his stoutest moccasins, the family usually knew that he was going on a hunting trip of some kind, perhaps into the rocky mountains or to the desert areas. Northern California Indians wore a one-piece, unsoled soft shoe. The sock-like deer-skin moccasin had a puckered seam up the front, and another seam up the heel (Yurok, Miwok, Hupa, Modoc style). The heel was made by drawing a leather thong through it. Tribes of southern California wore sandals of woven fibers wrapped around a looped frame. The sole was an inch thick. Hot, sun-dried earth could not be felt through these.

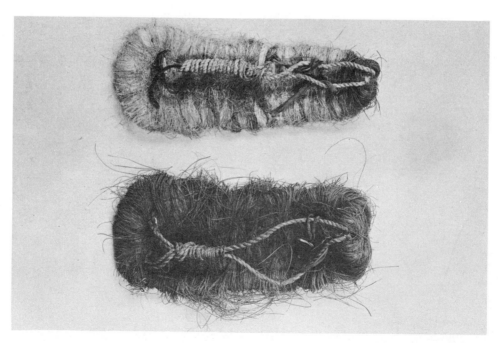

Fiber moccasins. (Robert H. Lowie Museum of Anthropology, University of California, Berkeley)

Leggings or high moccasins woven of tule fibers were used in some parts of northern California. Leggings for snowy weather were probably made of some kind of animal skin. Layers of soft grass in the bottom of them made walking easier and kept feet warmer.

When the weather was cold, rainy, or windy, more clothing was needed. Men, women, and children had deerskin blankets that they threw over their shoulders like a cape. Some wrapped the blanket around the body, over one arm and under the other and tied it in front. Soft sea otter fur was best to use but it was not so easy to get. Another kind of blanket was made of woven strips of rabbit fur. Such a blanket was worn in the daytime and used as a cover at night.

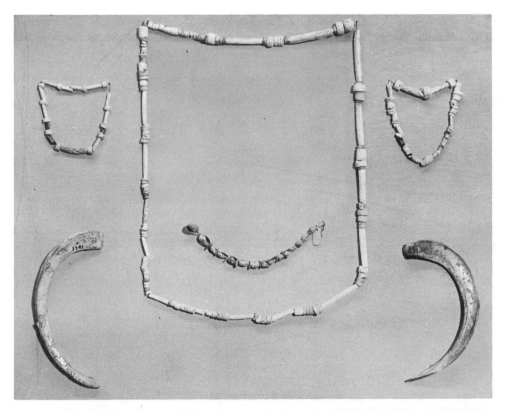

Ornaments of shell and bone. (Santa Barbara Museum of Natural History, Bosworth Lemere)

Chapter 5

HOUSES OF TULE, BRUSH,

AND BARK

Indians built houses which would seem a little strange to us. Houses had to be built with whatever material they could find and in ways that would fit their needs. There were no saws to cut down trees and nothing but stone tools to make planks.

Most of the Indians lived outdoors a good deal of the time even though houses were used as homes just as ours are for eating, sleeping, talking, working. In some areas the weather was very hot, while in parts of the north the weather was cold for several months of the year. Some houses were made of tule, some were made of rough bark planks, and still others were covered with earth. In desert areas the houses were little more than shelters from the hot sun. Some of the houses were large enough for several families; others were very small. Some were shaped like a dome, some like a cone, and some had a ridge-style roof. Notched ladders were used to climb into some of the houses. Others had doors so low that the Indians had to bend to get into them.

In the north where the Yurok and Hupa families lived, the winters were wet and cold. There were forests of oaks and pines in their area and so their houses were of tree-bark planks. The planks were split with a strong elkhorn wedge. If a fallen tree was found in the forest, this was used. If not, the tree had to be burned down by a fire set at the base. The Shastan family, also in the north, had much the same type of house except that a deep hole was dug and a plank roof placed over the top of it. This cellar-like house was cozy and warm in the winter months.

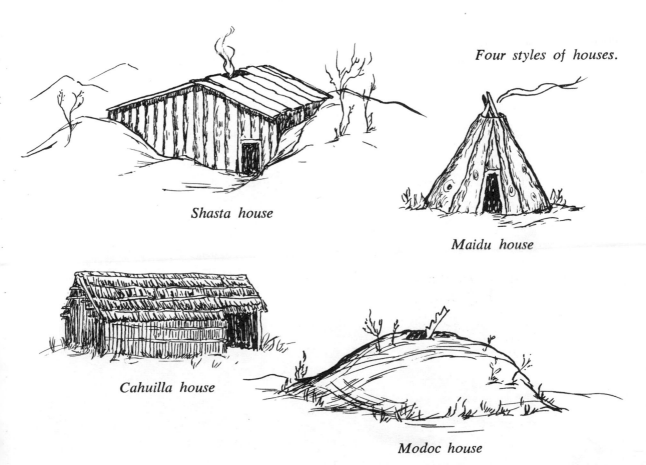

Four styles of houses.

Shasta house

Maidu house

Cahuilla house

Modoc house

In the center of the floor in these houses there was a small hole where the fire was made. Above the fire, one of the planks was raised to let the smoke out. Here during the long winter months the mother cooked the food and the family ate and worked.

Tribes to the south and east also had tree-bark houses. Theirs were cone-shaped and not so well made. The Sacramento Valley houses were mostly under the ground. Above the ground, the house was cone-shaped and covered with brush, not planks.

Many tribes such as the Chumash and the Yokuts had round, dome-like brush houses. First, men set poles into the ground in a circle. Inside the circle of poles a hole about two feet deep was dug. The tops of the poles were then bent together and tied with strips of leather or willow bark. Smaller poles were tied

Brush-covered house of the Shoshoneans. (Southwest Museum, Los Angeles)

The tule bed was covered with a skin blanket. (Arthur Barr Productions, Inc.)

crossways around the sides of the house. Women and children went to nearby marshes and gathered armloads of tule reed. The tule reed was woven into mats and fastened to the sides of the little house. An opening was left at the top to let in a little light and fresh air. A fire in the middle of the house kept everyone warm on cool nights. Wisps of smoke floated out through the hole left in the center of the roof. There was a small door on one side of the house, with a mat hung over it to keep out wind, cold, or rain. The extra dirt dug from the hole was put around the outside base of the house. This helped to keep the house warm and dry. In some areas where the weather was colder, the same kind of house was built except that mud was put over the tule mats or brush.

The Yokuts made beds by digging a hole in the dirt floor and filling it with dried tule grass. Some families spread tule mats on the floor near the center fire. Others piled mats around the inside walls and slept on them. Sometimes springy pine needles were placed under the mats to make the beds softer. Clothes, storage baskets, and other things that they owned and used were hung around the sides of the walls or on shelves dug into the earth. A string hammock was like a cupboard or closet where things could be stored. In the evening by the warm, cozy fire, the family sang and listened to stories told by the older members.

Most families had several small houses. They moved about in their own territory looking for food. Food-gathering times in summer and fall were like vacations. When they went up into the hills or mountains they gathered enough seeds and acorns to last until the next season. When they stayed in a place for a while, they put up a light brush-covered shelter, open at the sides and held up by four poles.

There was another kind of house in many villages called a sweat house (later called a *temescal*). It was given this name

Small house or sweat house of the Luiseño tribe. (Southwest Museum, Los Angeles)

because it was so warm inside that the Indians could sweat freely. All California tribes or family groups had such sweat houses except the Colorado River Indians and those who lived in the desert areas. They were hot enough without this kind of house, especially in the summer months. The sweat houses were used in several ways. It was a place used for curing certain ills but most of all it was a place to get clean. Indians believed that being clean gave them strength. A very hot fire was made in the center of the room. Since there was no smoke hole, the sweat house became hot and smoky. Men lay on the floor or sat by the fire and stayed there as long as they could stand the heat. When they were wet with perspiration they headed for the door. With a shout they rushed for the nearest stream and plunged into the cold water! It was agreed that the sweat house made them feel better and it certainly was a good way to keep clean. If near a stream or the ocean, Indians bathed almost every day. Sometimes a very large sweat house was built, called a "dance house." These were used as social halls for dancing, games, special celebrations or for visiting with one's friends.

Chapter 6

PLANTS THE INDIANS USED

Today, California's orchards and gardens produce enough food for the state, as well as for other states and even other countries. What did the Indians eat before there were cultivated plants? Except for the Yuman tribe, the California Indians never learned to plant and grow crops. Even though Indians fished in rivers, lakes, the ocean, and along the shores, and hunted wild game in the forests, most of their food came from plants that grew around them. A supply of food could be found with little work —acorns, seeds, nuts, fruits, roots, and leaves which could be cooked or eaten raw. The wonder is that they made such wide use of so many plants. If there was not enough of one kind of food, they looked for another. They moved from place to place within their territories as the various foods were ready to pick. In the spring there were plants such as clover and Indian's lettuce; in the summer there were fruits and berries; in the fall, acorns and seeds. The desert did not offer many foods but with careful searching some foods were found even there. A patient people, the Indians never hurried or worried very much. What they couldn't find one day, they found at another time in another place. Sometimes the Indians did not have certain foods in some seasons such as winter, but they did not starve for usually food had been stored away for such a time.

The Indians were lucky to find so many oak trees in California, especially along the coast and on both sides of the big central valley. Women were the food-gatherers. In the fall when the oaks had ripe acorns, women left their homes in the village, usually in a group to make the harvest task happier. Each woman wore a woven, basket-like cap. A net which held a basket was slung across her forehead. In her hand she carried a

Acorns were an important food. (Robert C. Frampton)

smaller basket to be filled with acorns and then emptied it into the larger net basket. The women laughed and sang as the baskets were filled to the brim with food for the months ahead. Women also wandered through the lowland plains and the foothill meadows when the grasses turned yellow. With seed-beaters they scooped tops of grasses or other seeds into shallow baskets. This time the net baskets were filled with seeds for use during the winter months.

When the acorns had dried the children helped crack them with stones. The dry acorn seed covering has a brown, papery skin like that of a peanut. This skin had to be stripped off. Then the acorns could be pounded into meal with a stone mortar and pestle. Often the women went to a large rock in which there were small scooped-out holes where they pounded the acorns. We can imagine that they enjoyed pounding in time to their singing or chatting. When they were not singing, they could talk over the latest village news.

After the pounding, the bitter taste (from tannic acid) had

Seed-beaters and seed-gathering baskets. (Robert H. Lowie Museum of Anthropology, University of California, Berkeley)

to be removed from the acorn meal. To do this a little hill of sand was made and the center scooped out. Large leaves were put in the bottom and the meal was placed on top of them. Water was poured over the meal many times. It seeped through the meal and down through the sand. Then the meal was no longer bitter and was ready to be made into a mush. Sometimes water was poured over the meal in a basket. A slower way was to bury the hulled acorns in a wet, swampy place for several months. Indians thought that this also took the bitter taste out of the acorns.

Now the sweetish, pink meal had to be cooked. There were no pots or pans, so the meal and water were put into a tightly woven basket. With a looped stick, hot stones were dropped into the water. Women had to stir the mush around and around as fast as they could so that holes would not be burned in the basket. Then the still bubbling hot mush was ready to be eaten.

Water was heated and food was cooked in baskets with hot stones. (*Arthur Barr Productions, Inc.*)

Another way was to bake or fry the mush on slabs of steatite or hot flat rocks.* The Indians liked this mush and probably used it the way we use bread.

In desert areas, pottery bowls were used for cooking over fires. Some of the Indians were lucky enough to have strong soapstone jars and bowls. Cooking in these was much easier. Meat, seeds, roots, and other foods were cooked in baskets. Fish and meat were often roasted in a deep pit filled with red-hot coals or sometimes on a stick held over the fire.

From the earth came all the good things the Indians had or needed and they lived well with all they found around them. They used seeds for food which were pounded in a stone grinding bowl (mortar) or on a slightly scooped-out, shallow grinding stone (later called a *metate*).** With another stone like a small rolling pin (Spanish name *mano* means hand) women ground seeds into meal. Seed meal was either eaten dry, pinch by pinch, or cooked like acorn mush or made into small cakes and roasted.

Another food came from mesquite bushes. Mesquite was a very important plant, especially to the desert tribes. It provided food, wood for building houses or fences, fibers for baskets, a black dye for pottery designs and tattooing, arrow shafts, and gum to chew. Mesquite also made strong digging sticks.

From the mesquite bushes hung long, pod-like beans. In a good year the ground was covered with the ripe pods. Brown pods were sweet and good to eat. Green pods could be picked from the trees in summer, dried and stored like acorns. When dried they were ground into a coarse meal. The meal was put into a pot or jar and soaked. If mixed with water it became a sweetish drink. The meal could be made into cakes and baked. Sometimes little hard balls made from mesquite meal provided the only food carried on a journey. The meal could also be

---

* Atole, *an important food, was used throughout California. It was a thick, soup-like food made from ground, leached acorns or a number of nut-like seeds.*
** *Cahuilla name for mortar and pestle was* ka-wa-val *and* pa-u-ul. Metate *and* mano *were called* mal-al *and* kak-ish.

cooked, stored in a pit and left for several weeks. From time to time water was poured on it. When ready to be eaten, the liquid was brown, thick and sweet like molasses. Among some tribes, the mesquite seeds were removed, ground into flour and made into a mush (Spanish name for the mush was *pinole*). The screw bean, much like the mesquite pods, was used in much the same way. When first picked, the screw bean had a sour or bitter taste but after cooking in oven pits for a long time, the pods had a sweet taste.

The *chia* (Spanish name for a kind of sage) had seeds in early summer. Indians called it *pa-sal*. It was one of the most widely known plants used by Indians and it still grows over most of California in dry, open places. Women gathered the seeds by beating the dried plant head over a tightly woven basket. If men brought in bundles of *chia* plants, they were put in a large pile and the seeds beaten off with seed-beaters or rods. The

Another food was the screw bean. (Robert C. Frampton)

Indians liked the chia *seeds more than almost anything else. (Robert C. Frampton)*

The seeds, fruit, and the stalks of the cactus were eaten. (Robert C. Frampton)

small, slippery, gray-brown seeds were liked by the Indians better than almost any other kind and they picked them in large amounts. Dried *pa-sal* or *chia* seeds, rich in oil, were pounded into meal and cooked.* It was said that one teaspoon of the meal was enough to keep from getting hungry for a whole day or more. When uncooked, the seeds were taken on trips. The seeds could be mixed with water to make a pleasant drink.

Mustard (tansy) is a plant still found throughout California. The tiny, red seeds were gathered by the Indians and used for food. The seeds were tossed in a tightly woven basket with hot coals until toasted and then ground. The seed meal had a rather peppery taste and was usually mixed with the meal from other seeds. The leaves were boiled or roasted and enjoyed much as we like mustard greens.

Cactus (*na-vit*) grows in the mountains and desert areas. Once, the seeds of the cactus (*mu-tal*), the fruit, and the stalks were eaten. A small cactus (*ma-nai*) which ripened in summer was very sweet. In some desert areas the flower buds and joints

* Pinole *was another staple food widely used.* Pinole *was a fine flour made by grinding* chia, *tansy mustard, or many of the grasses and annual flowering plants and was eaten dry or in some form of mush.*

were used after the sharp spines were removed. Then they were dried, stored, and boiled as needed. The fruits of the common tuna or Indian fig (cactus) were eaten raw after being peeled and the spines taken off. A good syrup was made by boiling the peeled fruits and straining out the seeds. Another use of the plants was to gather the cactus leaves (spines), and to cut them into strips to serve as a vegetable. The Indians gathered the fully ripe fruits and dried them. After the seeds were winnowed out, they were stored to be made into a flour (*atole* as it was later called).

Yucca (Spanish Bayonet) was very important as a food and as a fiber. It is still found on hillsides, in sandy canyons, and on desert slopes. The fruit with big, black seeds was picked when green. Roasted in hot coals, it had a taste somewhat like a baked green apple. When ripe, the fruit was sweet and juicy. The stem of the yucca was roasted in pits with hot coals. Fibers of the yucca had many uses: nets, baskets, mats, sandals, straps, cradles, rough-woven cloth and hairbrushes.

There are several kinds of mescal (Century plant, agave) which grow over a large part of the desert regions, chiefly in the rocky areas. The most important use of the mescal for the Indians was as food. In spring, the mescal flower buds begin to shoot up from the center of little rosettes. In the spring the Indians, in a group, camped for weeks while they gathered, cooked, and ate the mescal. A huge oven pit was dug in which a fire was built. When the pit was very hot, they took out the red-hot coals and laid a layer of agave leaves or grass over the ashes. The mescal heads were carefully laid over the grass in layers and finally a last layer of grass or agave leaves was put on top. The final step was to cover the pit with sand or earth. There the mescal heads were left to roast slowly until the next day. When they opened the pit and removed the leaves, the Indians found that the buds had become a brown, juicy mass and

Yucca was an important source of food and fiber. (Robert C. Frampton)

very sweet. Probably mescal hot from the oven was as tempting
and good as the hot sweet rolls we enjoy today. The supply had
to last for many months, however. Some was made into cakes
and dried for winter use. If there was more than enough, people
from neighboring territories were glad to trade their products
for such delicious cakes. A good, sweet drink was also made
by boiling pieces of the cake in winter. Young flower stems and
flower buds that had not opened were prepared in the same way.
As a fiber, mescal had some uses but not as many as yucca.
Charcoal of burned mescal or agave was used for tattooing

bluish black patterns pricked into the skin by cactus thorns.

Piñon or pine nuts, which we eat today, were used by many California Indians wherever pine trees could be found. This was usually on dry, rocky slopes and ridges, along the Sierra Nevada and in the mountains which border the Mojave Desert. Whole tribes traveled many miles to harvest the delicious pine nuts. The small pine cones were loosened from the trees with a forked stick. The tight little cones were piled in heaps and roasted until they popped open. Then the piñon nuts were shaken out, shelled, and eaten raw or roasted. They were as good as candy to Indians and they could be taken with them wherever they went and eaten anytime.

Islay (*yslaya*—the Indian name) or holly-leaved cherry had seeds or pits that were dried, ground into meal, and washed as acorn meal. This meal was not used for breadmaking but many

Indians were very fond of the good-tasting piñons that came from pine-tree cones. (Robert C. Frampton)

Agave was food for the desert tribes. (Rancho Santa Ana Botanic Garden, Claremont—M & M Carothers Photo)

tribes made it into a kind of soup. The fruit itself may have been used to make a drink.

Red berries of the *madrone* were eaten fresh but more often were cooked, dried, stored, and soaked in water until time of use. Sometimes the bluish marble-sized *manzanita* berries were mixed with the *madrone* berries. The Cahuilla tribe of southern California especially liked the *manzanita* berries (*is-wut*) that could be eaten fresh, or dried and stored to be made later into meal for mush or cakes. A drink was also made from the berries. The beautiful brownish wood was used in making houses or fences.

Bulbs found in the wet meadows that could be dug up with a sharp stick were used as food by many Indians. *Camas* was the most important bulb used. The bulbs were usually cooked in a hot pit for a day or two. When taken out they were soft, dark-ish brown, and very sweet. Some Indians liked to eat them hot from the pit. They must have tasted somewhat like roasted chestnuts. Most of the cooked bulbs were dried in the sun and made into cakes for later use (as with the mescal).

The common arrowhead or tule potato was harvested in late summer. This grew along the edge of ponds and slow streams. Indian women waded into the water and loosened the tubers (bulbs). They baked the tule potato as we do our potatoes and ate them whole or mashed.

Jojoba, a common shrub that grew on rocky hillsides, had large oily nuts. The nuts were eaten right from the bush or could be ground into a pleasant drink.

Of all the tribes, only the Mohaves and the Yumas grew any plants. Others probably thought that there were enough plants growing wild. In later years the mission padres taught the Indians how to grow and harvest many crops.

Women gathered food plants but men brought in meat. Some deer were caught in brush-covered pits along deer trails. A deer hunter took a stuffed deer head and placed it on his own. In this way the deer was fooled into believing that the Indian was another deer. When he came close, the arrow whizzed from the bow and down went the deer!

Rabbit was the day-to-day meat and there always seemed to be plenty of it. Rabbits were not only good for food but their fur was useful. They were caught in pits as well as with bow and arrow. Another way was to throw a curved rabbit stick and hit the rabbit. Rabbit sticks could be thrown straight and hard and were also used to catch birds. Another way to catch rabbits

When deer-hunting, the Indian tried to look and act like a deer. (Arthur Barr Productions, Inc.)

was with nets. Whole families of Indians spread out in a line. Hunters beat at the shrubs and drove rabbits into the long, low nets. Rats, mice, and squirrels were trapped also. All of them were either roasted over a fire or made into a soup. Indians did not eat coyotes or grizzly bears. Both of these animals were respected, for the Indians thought the coyote was supposed to be an evil spirit, the bear a good spirit.

When food was scarce the Indians ate grasshoppers, worms,

The harpoon that looked like a spear was pushed forward, not thrown. (Exhibit, Los Angeles County Museum)

giant ants, or caterpillars if enough of them could be found. These were unusually delicious when roasted. Large roasted grasshoppers were a favorite food! We know that tribes in the south ate snakes and certain lizards to add to their variety of foods.

Plenty of fish were found in the rivers and ocean. Shellfish and mussels were taken from the sea or gathered along the shore. Sometimes whales came near enough to be pulled ashore. Then the fishermen of the village took to their boats with pointed harpoons. When they were lucky every family in the village had a feast! Besides fish there were many clams and crabs. Rivers were full of all kinds of fish, especially salmon in the northern streams. When salmon came up the rivers in the spring many were caught. This was a time for feasting and celebration.

Nets were used more than fishhooks for catching fish. On the

Different kinds of fishhooks and how they were made. (Exhibit, Santa Barbara Museum of Natural History—Bosworth Lemere)

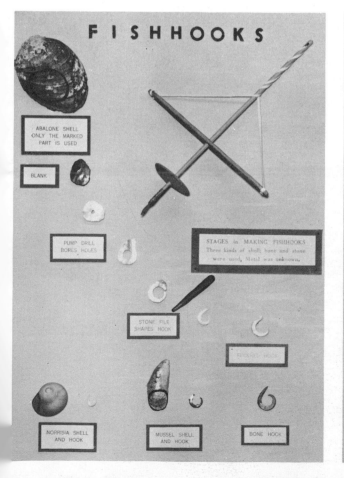

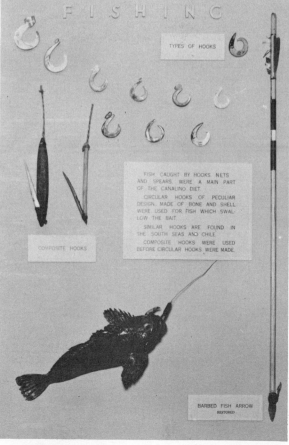

southern coast in deep waters, shell fishhooks were used, and sometimes a harpoon that looked like a spear. The long slender shaft was pushed forward, not thrown. A heavier harpoon that was thrown was used by the northwest tribes to catch sea lions.

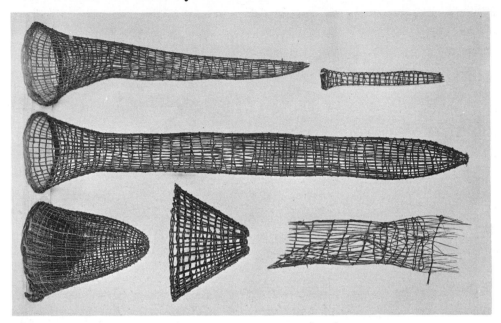

Fish traps. (Robert H. Lowie Museum of Anthropology, University of California, Berkeley)

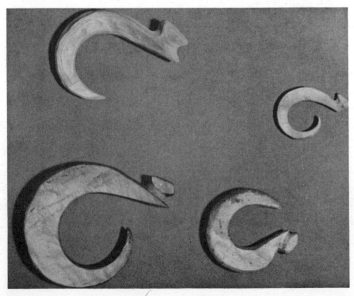

Fishhooks made from shells. (Southwest Museum, Los Angeles)

Large nets and dip nets were known to all the Indians. They knew the best kind to use whether they were catching fish in streams or from the seashore. Nets had floats of wood or tule stems. Notched flat rocks made by Indians have been found. We believe that they were "sinkers" used to stretch and hold the nets in the water.

Indians liked to flavor their food with salt when they could find it. Salt plants grew in northern California near the redwood area. Here the Indians gathered the big leaves and stems of the salt plant. These were spread in the sun until they wilted and then they were rolled up into balls. The balls were put on redwood slabs and slowly heated until they changed into ashes which were almost pure salt. In the Mendocino area there were salt springs around which crusts of salt covered the ground and plants. Indians for miles around made journeys to get salt there

A favorite drink was made from the lemonade berry. (Robert C. Frampton)

Indians liked to eat raw onions. (Robert C. Frampton)

and took enough to last them for at least a year.

We know something of what the Indians ate by the things that have been found buried. In places where villages once stood, huge areas mark places where fires had burned. Bones of deer, sea lions (or seals), rabbits, and birds show that these are some of the things they ate. Old shell mounds tell us that some of their food was taken from the ocean. Old grinding bowls, stone grinding slabs (*metates*), tools and jars—or pieces of them—tell us some of the ways they must have prepared their food. Indians today still use some of the same plants their forefathers used, and others can remember having eaten many of them when they were young.*

* See Addenda: "Some of the Important Plants Used for Medicine," "Other Uses for Plants by the Indians," "Plants Used in Basketmaking and for Dyes."

Chapter 7

THE INDIAN FAMILY AT HOME

The mother of the family was a hard worker. From sunrise to sunset she had plenty to do; her tasks never seemed to be finished. She was up at daybreak to get water and a few sticks of wood for the fire. A light breakfast was eaten by the family and then each member went to his day's work.

Most of the day the mother spent pounding meal or gathering and preparing any other kinds of food. She took the girls with her when she went to the woods nearby to find ripe berries, juicy bulbs, or sweet-smelling herbs. Their sharp eyes helped the mother to find plants they knew were good for food. When the mother did have time to sit down, her hands were not idle. Baskets and other useful things for the family had to be made. No

All enjoyed the delicious mush. (Arthur Barr Productions, Inc.)

one told her what to do; she knew all too well.

Men also arose soon after the sun came up. After breakfast they were ready to start their day's work. They did the heavy work of gathering wood for building and finding stones for mortars. Some days the father of the family went with net, spear, or bow and arrow to get meat or fish. When the father of the family had time to spend at home, there were many things to be made—everything from new houses and canoes to stone tools and ornaments. In the afternoon after going to the sweat house, he liked to sit in the sun with his village friends and have a game or talk over their plans for the village people.

In the evening the family had the main meal of the day. The father ate slowly as he talked to his family about what he had done that day. The mother and the children showed respect by being silent. After that he was ready for a good night's sleep.

When all was quiet in the little house, the mother or grandmother, if there was one, sat with the children around the fire. This was a good story time. The mother had a sort of singsong story she told. She liked to tell of the places she could remember that meant something to her—the mountains, the high trees, the dancing waterfalls. Grandmother's stories were more exciting for she knew many animal tales. The bear, she told them, was the first one to live on earth. He was a powerful animal who should be respected. Children liked most to hear about the coyote, the clever animal that was always playing tricks. After the tiny light of the fire died down, there was nothing to do but go to sleep.

Indian children did their share of the work in the home. A daughter would help to care for the smaller children in the family. It was not unusual for her to carry a baby brother or sister strapped in a cradle on her back. Girls learned to do most of the things around the house that the mothers did. They started making baskets when quite young, small ones at first. Both the mother and grandmother taught the girls how to pound in the mortar and cook their simple food.

Even though there were no schools there were many things that both boys and girls had to learn. Boys were taught by their fathers to make bows and small tools. They learned how to skin deer, rabbits, or other animals. Sometimes the boys climbed into the leafy trees and brought down tiny eggs from birds' nests. Fathers led their sons into the valleys and up the cliffs of the canyons when they went hunting and fishing. The father or grandfather taught them how to throw the curved stick to catch a rabbit.

The father knew the land almost bush by bush, stone by stone, that belonged to the village and to the territory of his tribe. He had been taught this by his father. It was said that each Indian knew his own territory "by the soles of his feet" for he had gone over it so many times. It was important that the sons

Curved rabbit sticks.

of the family know all about the tribal territory, too. When boys grew older they were taught the songs, dances, and beliefs of the tribe. There were no books, of course, and so they had to have good memories.

Boys were given many harmless tests to prove their bravery. They also ran many miles so that their legs would be strong and they would be healthy.

Indian parents loved their children very much. Part of a child's training was how to behave. Some of the rules were:

Be good to older people
Tell the truth
Do not get angry
Be polite to everyone
Speak softly
Be brave and do not be afraid

They were told that if they did these things they would "grow old in good health." The older men said, "You will be able to tell your children about these things."

Chapter 8

BOATS, BOWS, AND TOOLS

Indian men were always busy doing other things besides building houses, going hunting, and fishing. They were very clever with their hands. Much of their time was spent building boats and making tools. In the beginning these early-day people had no iron or other metal. There were no axes, saws, knives, hammers, or nails. Once again we find that the Indians had to make what they could with the materials they had.

All the coastal Indians and those along rivers or lakes had to have boats. Two materials were used: wood and tule. Boats had to be used on swift, tumbling rivers as well as on quiet lakes. Others were used near the seashore but the strongest and best ones were used on the open sea.

These crude awls had many uses.

The Chumash made better boats than any other Indian tribe. (Santa Barbara Museum of Natural History, Bosworth Lemere)

Indians in the northwest built very strong redwood canoes although they looked heavy and clumsy. This kind of canoe was dug out from half a redwood log, and was square on the ends and round on the bottom. Seats for the paddlers were carved in the log. Long, heavy paddles were used both as paddles for rowing and for pushing the boat through the water. In the northeast, boats of pine, cedar, or fir were shaped by burning or chopping the logs with a sharp stone.

The wooden seagoing canoes of the Chumash were the best ones made in California or even in the United States. The Chumash painted their boats and often put designs of bright colors on them. This plank boat, or *tomolo,* as it was called, could be used in the rough waters of the ocean. It was used along the shore from Point Concepción to San Diego and across to the Santa Barbara Islands. Island Indians used them to visit the mainland. When a boatload of Indians came paddling to the mainland shore, village children ran shouting to meet them. Village people were excited as they gathered around to greet the visitors. Children had a happy time when their fathers took them fishing in the *tomolos.*

Chumash Indians "sewed" the planks together (view of bottom of boat). (Southwest Museum, Los Angeles)

The Chumash boats were made of split planks that had been scraped and smoothed. Holes were drilled or burned along the edges of each plank. Indians "sewed" the planks together with strong cords. Black, sticky tar or asphalt found along beaches was used to seal the seams and holes. The boats had double paddles. With them the men could shoot through the water. Explorers were surprised to see such wonderful boats and said that they "seemed to fly through the water." Such boats were twelve to twenty-two feet long and could carry from two to twelve people.

For traveling on the bays, a light tule boat was all that was needed. Even these boats could be paddled for some distance. Almost all the tribes used them. Bundles of tule were formed into flat boats, very long and high at each end. The tule boats were so light that they floated high on top of the water. Tule boats moved so quietly through the water that fish were not

Tule boats were made from long bundles of tule tied together with plant-fiber string. (Arthur Barr Productions, Inc.)

frightened away. The several men who went in them paddled with their feet while they were busy catching fish with nets or spears.

A few bundles of tule tied together into a raft was enough to keep it afloat. The small tule raft was "poled" rather than paddled, and could go short distances in still waters.

Some of the tribes lived near small streams and therefore did not need boats. If women and children wished to cross a stream, they used very large baskets or, in the south, large pots. Men waded into the water and pushed the baskets or pots across the narrow river.

As boats were important to Indian life, so were bows and arrows, and the men made many of them. The best bows were made of wood from the elder, laurel, and bay trees. The very finest ones were made of juniper wood. Wide strips of deer sinew were used for backing the bows, these being attached with glue made from deer's horns and hoofs. When the bows were finished, they were usually painted and decorated with designs.

If possible, arrow shafts were made from the heart of the button willow tree. However, many of the California Indian arrows were made in two parts: a long cane-like (*carrizo*) grass and a hardwood foreshaft that carried the point. Indians were clever about making the slender shafts very straight. First they made a groove in a flat stone. The stone was heated until very hot. The arrow shaft was soaked in water for a short time and run through the groove of the hot stone. In this way the arrow shaft was steamed until it was very straight.

Arrow straighteners. (Robert H. Lowie Museum of Anthropology, University of California, Berkeley)

72

After this, the arrow shaft was ready for the arrowhead or arrow point. Arrow points had to be of the hardest and finest stones that could be found. Indians liked best the shiny, black, hard volcanic glass called obsidian. The maker of arrow points shaped the obsidian or other hard rock with a stone tool, chip-

Any size or kind of arrow point needed by the hunter could be slipped into the main shaft of the arrow. (Arthur Barr Productions, Inc.)

Arrow points and spear points. (Santa Barbara Museum of Natural History—Bosworth Lemere)

ping them into shape bit by bit. This was not easy and took great care and patience. The base of the point was so notched that it could be fastened to the arrow shaft. As he bound the point to the shaft with sinew, the Indian chewed the sinew to make it soft. When the sinew was dry, the point was fastened even more securely with asphalt. Feathers were split and bound to the other end of the shaft. When bound in a spiral, the arrow could sail a long distance through the air. The bowstrings were made of twisted sinew or very strong plant fiber. Arrows were carried in a skin bag with the hide side turned in to protect the arrows. Men of all tribes were good arrow makers. They knew that fine arrows and bows were needed for hunting or for fighting if that

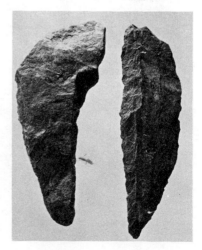

All they had to shape the steatite bowls were hard, pointed stones. (Southwest Museum, Los Angeles)

was necessary. The Yurok made such fine bows and arrows that other tribes were glad to either buy or trade to get them. Larger points were made for spears but they were not used very much.

Narrow, thin pieces of stone were used for borers to make holes in various objects such as beads. Hammers and axes were made from hard stones. A tough, solid rock was best for mortars, pestles, drills, and tools. Obsidian and hard flint stone were flaked into knives or blades used for skinning animals. Sharp-edged razor clam shells were also made into knives. Wedges or chisels were made from deer's horns and, among the Chumash, whale bones were used. Pipes for smoking were shaped from soapstone (steatite) or from certain other soft

Yurok acorn-gruel spoons made from elk antlers.

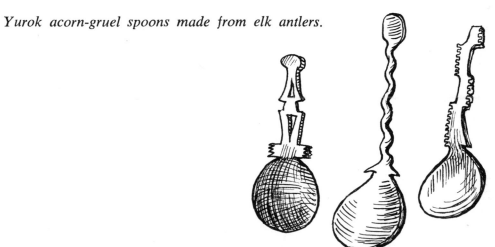

stones and woods. Needles and flutes were made from bones. Spoons and cooking paddles were of wood or deer's horns. Curved, wooden rabbit sticks had to be carefully shaped. Many hours of work were necessary to make all these things.

Nets of all sizes were used for fishing in fresh waters and still bays. The material for them was made from bark fibers or the outside fibers of Indian hemp and milkweed. The pulp was pounded to remove the fiber. Then the Indian would twist and roll the fibers up and down along his legs until a strong string

It took many hours of work to shape rock into bowls. (Santa Barbara Museum of Natural History, Bosworth Lemere)

was made. In the Shastan tribe area and in the northwest, irises grew and from them came thin, tough fibers for nets. The fibers were hard to get but the string made from them was thin and tough. Agave fibers made a course, stiff string. Sometimes the sharp spine at the tip of agave leaf was left on a string of agave fiber to make a perfect needle and thread! Grapevine was used for tying large articles.

The sharp spine and fiber of the agave made a good needle and thread. (Robert C. Frampton)

Charmstones, pendants, and ornaments of many kinds were shaped from smooth, well-polished stone. Not the least important things that the men made were fishhooks from shells of various kinds. Men were also the fire-makers. Fire was made by striking two pieces of hard stone together, or by a drill twirled by hand, until a spark flew out and was caught in a small pile of tinder or dried sticks and grass.

Indian men had to spend many hours hunting, gathering materials, and making boats, tools, weapons, and other necessities of everyday life.

Chapter 9

CLEVER HANDS AND NIMBLE FEET

Baskets and Basketmaking

Indian women spent many hours weaving baskets. They must have enjoyed the art of basketmaking, for the weaving of materials, colors, and designs show their skill. They made many kinds since baskets were important to their way of life. Baskets were various sizes, from small treasure baskets, baby carriers, seed-beaters, and cooking baskets, to large food storage ones. Some were woven closely and some loosely—each kind for a different use. With few materials and many hours of patient work, baskets of great beauty were made.

Baskets were either twined or coiled. Most Indians used only one of these methods, but some of the California women (Yuki,

Maidu, Yokuts) used both. Twined baskets were made by all Californians, but the northern tribes wove them especially well.

Twining is much like weaving. As the women wove the soft materials in and out between stiff rods or ribs (like an um-

Soft materials were twined in and out between the stiff rods. (Arthur Barr Productions, Inc.)

brella), they pulled the ribs upward to form the sides of the basket. The ribs were usually small hazel or willow roots, and they used strips of root from pine, redwood, or spruce trees for the twining material. They twined the strips tightly around each rib so that the basket would be tight and firm. Some of these twined baskets were loosely woven for carrying baskets, seed-beaters, traps, baby cradles, or for draining water through meal.

Coiling is more like sewing or stitching. Basket weavers who coiled made a start with one or more long thin reeds or a small bundle of long straws. Each row was sewed to the one before, row after row, around and around until the basket was the right size and shape. There were no needles, of course, so sharp bone awls were used to make a hole for each stitch. The basket was finished by stitching twice around the top coil. Then the extra

The Pomo women wove feathers along the rims of the beautifully made baskets. (Santa Barbara Museum of Natural History—Bosworth Lemere)

stitching material was cut off with a stone knife. You can imagine how proud the Indian woman was when her beautiful basket was completed!

Baskets were usually shaped like rounded bowls, some large and some small. In the south, baskets were made with a shoulder

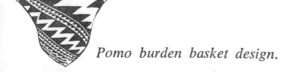

Pomo burden basket design.

and with a small neck. A few tribes wove baskets with no shoulders which were called "bottle neck" baskets. Some women's caps were tightly woven and were made round to fit the head. The caps of the southern California Indians were cone-shaped. Mats were loosely woven or twined like the baskets. Baby-car-

Types of cradles. (Robert H. Lowie Museum of Anthropology, University of California, Berkeley)

The Mono women made baskets of great beauty. (Santa Barbara Museum of Natural History—Bosworth Lemere)

rying cradles were of many styles, mostly of the lying-down kind. The Pomo wove a sitting-up type of cradle.

The Pomo women were the finest basketmakers in the United States. Their baskets were works of art. The Santa Barbara Chumash made fine ones also. Both the fine weaving and the designs were extremely well done. The Pomo baskets were different from others. Pomo women wove bright, soft feathers in and out all over the basket. The smallest baskets looked like a downy hummingbird's nest! They even wove lids for their baskets, as did the Chumash women. There were tribes that wove

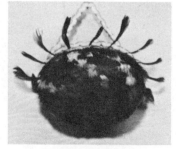

Tiny feathers were woven into the Pomo gift baskets. (Santa Barbara Museum of Natural History—Bosworth Lemere)

Baskets were important to them and they wove many kinds. (Robert H. Lowie Museum of Anthropology, University of California, Berkeley)

Some baskets had woven lids.
(Santa Barbara Museum of Natural
History—Bosworth Lemere)

a few feathers along the rims of baskets or strung shells that dripped along the sides. All these fine baskets were famous and were worth a good deal in trading. You can imagine that Indian women had a happy time as they worked on their baskets and visited together.

The Colorado River Indians made the poorest baskets. For the most part, theirs were loosely woven traps for wild animals

The bark of the redbud was peeled off and used for the red designs. (Rancho Santa Ana Botanic Garden, Claremont—M & M Carothers Photo)

Women took great care in finding the right grasses, roots, and stems for their baskets. (Arthur Barr Productions, Inc.)

or fish. The best baskets they had came to them in trade from neighboring tribes, the Diegueño and the Cahuilla.

One can well imagine the many hours it took to gather all the materials needed for basketmaking.* Women wandered through the woods near the village looking for grasses, roots, and stems useful for basket designs. Dyes for the colored designs came from plants also. All but the black were made with grass or reeds. Designs made with grass were light brown at first and became darker as they aged. Reeds were soaked in mud or dyed in berry juice to make the desired colors. Redbud, which gave

* See Addenda: "Plants Used in Basketmaking and for Dyes."

Yokuts basket designs.

Flies

Flies

Deer foot

Water snake markings

Deer foot

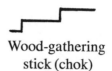
Wood-gathering
stick (chok)

Arrow points

Tied in the middle

Crooked

Arrow point

Crooked

Crooked

Rattlesnake markings

Millipede

Rattlesnake markings

King snake markings

King snake markings

Rattlesnake markings

86

Rattlesnake design basket. (Southwest Museum, Los Angeles)

the red color, was the plant most used. White, black, and some red dyes were made from the alder tree. Black stems of certain ferns made fine black designs. "Overlay" designs were made by twining the design on the outside of the basket. Coiled baskets had designs both inside and outside.

Weaving and design were taught to girls by their mothers. For this reason, the baskets and designs of each family group

The designs in some baskets did not always join because the designs were very difficult to make. (Southwest Museum, Los Angeles)

were about the same through the years. The designs had meanings and told stories known only to the women of each tribe. The designs ran in straight or broken bands around the baskets. Some had triangles, stars, birds, animals, or flowers. A design that ran around the basket like a snake was called the rattlesnake design. The Pomo women believed that the basketmaker who completely closed her design would become blind, so women left a break in their designs instead of joining them together and this break was called a *dau* (Pomo word).

Pottery

Basketmaking is an older art than pottery and few California Indians except those in desert areas made any pottery. Even this pottery was not too well made but just as good mush was cooked in them as in the decorated pots of other tribes. The Yuma, Mohave, and Colorado River tribes made pottery that was good enough for their daily needs: cooking and food bowls and pots, water and storage jars.

When making jars, crushed rock was mixed with clay and this mixture became dullish red when baked. The wet clay was first rolled into long, sausage-shaped pieces. A flat pancake of clay was made as a base for each jar or pot. Then the rolls of wet clay were coiled on top of the base, one roll on top of the other, around and around until the jar was formed. It was patted and

Cahuilla painted storage jar.

Mohave bowl and ladle with "rain" and "fish backbone" designs.

Mohave pottery bowl with "cottonwood leaf and rain" design.

shaped with the fingers and with a small smooth stone. The pots were then ready to be dried in the sun. Most of the pots had very simple designs painted on them. The last step was to bake the jars in a bed of hot coals to make them hard and strong.

Dancing

Indians had many kinds of dances. There was a dance when a baby was born and a mourning dance when anyone in the village died. There were hunting dances, wedding dances, thanksgiving dances, and dances when boys and girls became young men and women. Many dances had to do with religion because dancing to the Indians was a form of prayer.

When spring came, bringing the cheery songs of birds, green hills, and many-colored flowers, it was a perfect time for dancing. When the juicy new clover was ready for picking and eating, Indians danced for joy. In northern California, Indians were glad when they heard a shout through the village of *"Ne-peg-wuh"* ("the salmon"), for that meant that the first salmon of the season had been seen. That night there was sure to be a "salmon dance."

In the fall, when the acorns and seeds were ripe, Indians had a thanksgiving dance. They also celebrated the beginning of the hunting season. Seated around the fire, old men of the tribe told of the fat elk and deer that had been caught and dried for the winter months. Besides the meat, everyone knew that the animal skins would give them warm capes and blankets. Women told of the many baskets of acorns and seeds they had gathered and stored. Each told of the things he had done or made. After the stories and feasting, the dancing began.

At some time during the year, usually the latter part of summer, there was a dance for the dead. A large pile of wood and food to be burned was made in a certain place in the village. In the evening around the fire there was mourning for all those who had died during the year. New clothing and baskets were brought as gifts to the dead. As the Indians danced, one gift after another was thrown into the flames. They danced faster and faster, crying louder and louder until all the gifts had been burned.

Music

No matter how simply the Indians lived, each tribe had some kind of music. Music to them was not a tune but more a humming or low, slow chanting in time to the stamping of feet or the clapping of hands. Their voices had a singsong quality to them. Tribal history and stories were told in song and many of them had a religious meaning.

Men made flutes of bone or wood, some large and some quite small. Only a few notes could be played on any of them. The musician played by blowing across the holes of his flute. If a man could "sniff" or blow air from his nose across the holes, he was thought to be a good player. A wooden whistle used at ceremonies was so shrill that it could be heard above the chanting of the people.

Several kinds of rattles were used for dancing ceremonies.

Men made flutes that would play a few notes. (Santa Barbara Museum of Natural History—Bosworth Lemere)

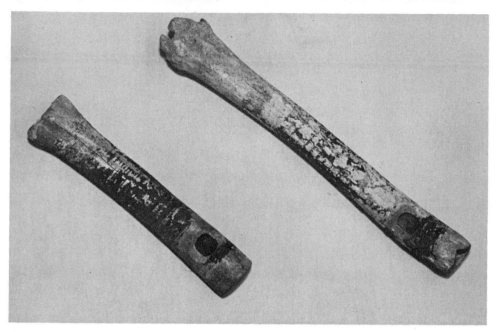

One rattle was made of two shells put together with cherry seeds or small rocks inside. Another kind was made by tying deer hoofs on strings to a stick. Sometimes a man tapped on his bowstring and this made a sort of "twang." Medicine men had rattles made from dried cocoons filled with stones. A claker or rhythm stick was a split stick which made a rhythmic sound when beaten against the hand. A "bull roarer" was a wooden slab on a string

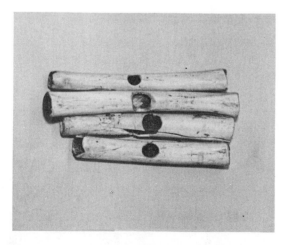

Some of the flutes were quite small. (Santa Barbara Museum of Natural History—Bosworth Lemere)

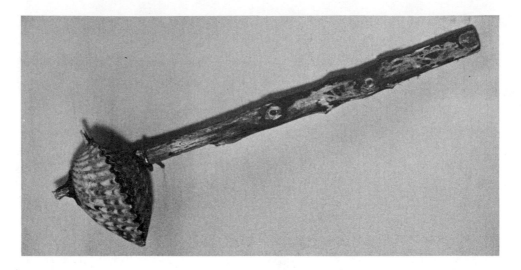

that made a whirring sound when swung around in the air. The Luiseño tribe used the "bull roarer" to announce the arrival of visitors. A leader of the Cahuilla tribe used it to call people to the front of the ceremonial house to see the Eagle Dance. Drums were unknown in the earlier years except as an Indian thumped on a log with his hands or a heavy stick.

You can imagine Indians outdoors on summer evenings, as they danced, sang, and told the old stories that they had heard over and over again.

Medicine men had cocoon rattles.

Pictographs and Petroglyphs

Pictures that are painted on rocks are pictographs and those carved on rocks are petroglyphs. Hundreds of Indian petroglyphs still remain but there are only about seventy sites where pictographs have been found. Years have been spent in searching for these pictographs in mountain canyons and caves. Most of them have been found in the Shoshonean and Chumash areas. The ones found in caves have been better protected but even so, many of them are fading away. Until recently, people did not know their value and many were destroyed. Pictures of the pictographs have been made with great care so that a record of them will not be lost.

The pictographs were painted in shades of red and brown and black and white. It is believed that the red and brown colors were made from colored rocks or ores (such as iron oxide) that had been ground into powder and mixed with animal fat for an oil base. There are many places in the Chumash area where limestone is found and probably the white came from this kind of rock. Perhaps the black came from charcoal left in old fire holes. The red colors soaked into the rocks and so the red designs have lasted better than the others.*

The crude designs found are of men, animals, insects, the sun and stars, zigzag lines, triangles, circles. The designs most likely were painted on the rocks with fingers, with a pointed stick, or with some plant fiber that was frayed like a brush on the end. The petroglyphs that have been deeply pecked or chipped into rocks with sharp stone tools have not changed throughout the years. But others have been worn by weather and are difficult to see.

What do all these designs mean? How old are they? This is still a puzzle. The answers to these questions died with the Indians who made them. It is believed that they were made by medicine men who wished to tell others their thoughts. They

* See endsheets for facsimile painting of a pictograph found in a cave in the Chumash area.

may have had something to do with special ceremonies or they may have had a religious meaning. To us, however, they appear to be a kind of Indian art. Some pictographs have been found that show moons with lines between them, which may have been a way of counting time. It is possible that they could have been maps of trails leading to hunting grounds, as many are found along old hunting trails. Wherever found and in whatever condition, they should be prized and saved.

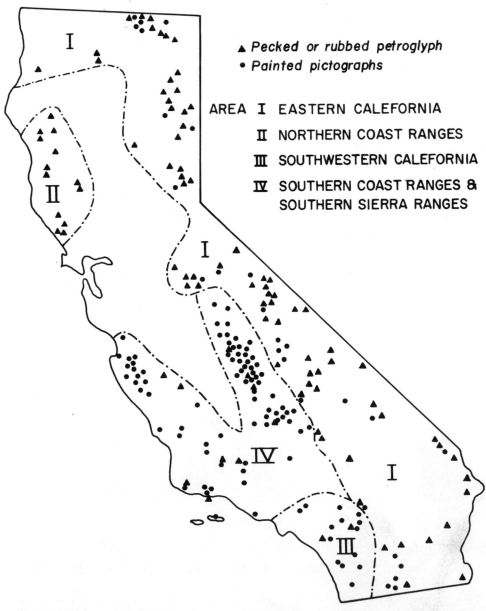

▲ Pecked or rubbed petroglyph
• Painted pictographs

AREA I   EASTERN CALEFORNIA
     II   NORTHERN COAST RANGES
     III SOUTHWESTERN CALEFORNIA
     IV   SOUTHERN COAST RANGES &
          SOUTHERN SIERRA RANGES

Some of the places where pictographs and petroglyphs may be found.

This map* gives the pictographs/petroglyphs locations by area in California and the styles found in each area. Many designs, especially the simple ones, are widespread throughout the state.

AREA I

This area is roughly that part of California lying east of the crest of the Sierra Nevada. This area has petroglyphs (pecked or chipped) in the following simple designs.

| Mountain sheep | Hand or foot prints | Snakes | Circular chains | Circle grid |

* Report of the Archeological Survey, May 1, 1949, Department of Archeology, University of California, Berkeley.

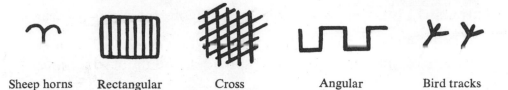

Sheep horns   Rectangular   Cross   Angular   Bird tracks
grids   hatching   lines

Rain symbol

AREA II

The northern Coast Range area has rubbed groove petroglyphs found on the faces of rocks or exposed bedrock such as steatite. The most distinct feature of this area is the cup-shaped depressions (average is about 3 inches in diameter and less than 1 inch deep). Petroglyph designs are variations of these cup-shaped designs.

Cup depressions

AREA III

The southwestern area has mostly red painted pictographs of geometrical designs in line arrangements, especially chains of diamonds and parallel rows of zigzag lines. These pictographs are found on the vertical faces of isolated boulders.

Diamond chain   Zigzag rows

This is a region where pictographs are elaborate and in several colors. Red is most common but yellow, black and white are often found. The designs are large and usually occur on the vertical faces of rock cliffs.

Cogged wheel

Round bands   Human   Human   Fur pelt   Centipede
of color

Chapter 10

INDIANS AT PLAY

No one, whether young or old, can work all the time. The Indians knew that play was important too. Almost every village had a space either large or small where games of various kinds could be played. Sometimes one village played against those in a neighboring village and this was good fun for all. Those who did not play, both old and young, stood along the sides of the field to watch. You can imagine that the watchers jumped up and down and became just as excited as we do at a game!

Men liked to play a game called "shinny." The playing area was set up a little like our football field with goal posts at each end. The players, from two to fifteen men, lined up facing each other. With a curved stick a wooden ball was driven down the field toward the goal post. The team whose ball got to the post by the fewest strokes was the winner. If there were only two players they raced down the field side by side. This fast game was fun for both watchers and players. Lucky was the player whose head was not batted instead of the ball!

The hoop and pole game was played the most, except in the northwest area. It was played with a small hoop or a circle of willow branch wound with a fiber string, and with a long pole. The pole when thrown was supposed to fall through the rolling hoop. Each time it did a point was made and so many points made a game.

The Miwok women played a game something like our basketball. A deerskin ball was stuffed with grass or something else soft. Each player had two baskets shaped like seed-beaters, one a little larger than the other. Players stood in a line. When the ball was thrown into the air, each player tried to catch it in the large basket. Whoever did put the smaller basket over the ball so that it would not roll out. Then she raced with it down the field to the goal.

Sometimes members of the village played a "tug of war" game. Men and boys were on one side and women and girls on the other. Each side tried to pull the other one over a center line. It was a great joke when men let go of their end. Then the women and girls went laughing and tumbling to the ground!

These were field games but Indians liked sitting-down games also. Guessing games were often played by men, dice games by women. One sitting-down game was something like our game of "Button, Button, Who Has the Button?" This game was sure to be played whenever Indians met together in a group. Not all tribes played the game alike but the idea was about the same. In this game there were two or more players on each side. An older man sat near the players to settle quarrels and see to it that they did not cheat. Each side had singers and as the game went

Everyone seemed to like the hoop and pole game. (Arthur Barr Productions, Inc.)

on, they swayed and sang loudly. They must have been much like our cheerleaders at a game! The singers were supposed to bring good luck to their side.

Two sticks or bones small enough to be held in a man's hand were used. One was plain and one was marked by a string around it or painted with a band in the center. The holders of the bones or sticks hid their hands under a skin or blanket. The pieces were passed one to the other. The side that was guessing pointed quickly to the hand it thought had the marked stick or bone. If right, it was the other side's turn to do the hiding. If not, the first side hid the piece again. Sometimes black and white pieces were used and players had to guess who had the white one. Ten or twelve sticks were stuck into the ground. Each time a side guessed right, it was given one of the sticks. The game was won when one side or the other won all the counting sticks. Games like this lasted for hours, sometimes all night, and there was much betting as to which side would be the winner. The Mohaves had a different way of playing. One player stuck a small stick into one of four little piles of sand. In which sand pile was the stick hidden? That was the game.

Among Indian women dice games took the place of today's card games. Women dressed in their nicest skirts and fancy woven basket caps. On went their very best necklaces, bracelets, and earrings. Then they were ready to go to a "dice party." The dice were round pieces of shell, sticks, tiny rocks, or nut shells that had been filled with tar. Whatever was used, a number of dots or designs were painted on one side of the dice. If the side that had the dots on it came up, so many points were counted. If the other side came up there were no points.

Many tribes played a ring and pin game. Rings were put on a string and fastened to a pointed stick. The game was to toss up the rings and catch them on the stick. Rings were made of many things such as acorns with the center pushed out to make a hole, or shells with holes in the center.

Nearly all games played by grown people were gambling games. They would bet with everything from shell money and deerskins to baskets and beads. They would even lose their food or houses if they bet and did not win.

Women liked dice games.
(Chemehuevi filled shells)

Young Indian children loved to play. There were no schools, of course, and so life was like a long vacation for them until they began to grow up, at which time there was work for them to do.

Girls had dolls that would seem strange to our girls today. Some of the dolls were only a deerskin wrapped around a stick. Some were of grass and others were made of clay. Nearly all the little girls had tiny doll cradles made like those for the baby of the family.

Boys were given small bows and arrows. They did not really use them but only pretended that they were hunting. They liked tops made with acorns that had little sticks in them. Boys tried to see whose top would spin the longest.

Small children played a game something like our hopscotch. They tried to see how far they could hop on one leg. The Miwok children played a game of hide-and-go-seek and also tag. The Pomo children played a game in a ring using a fiber ball. When a player batted the ball out of the ring he was "out." The last player to be "out" was the winner. Children were lucky who lived near the ocean, lakes, or a river, for they could go swimming.

It is interesting to find that many of the games we have today are much like those once played by children of that time.

Acorn tops.

Chapter 11

SOMETHING OF VALUE:
TRADING AND SHELL MONEY

The Indians had no money as we know it today, but they had to have something that could be used for trading with one another. Their money was made from things around them that had the most value. They used shells for money, not just any shells but special ones. Near the seashore the common shell was the clamshell and so their cheapest money (as we would think of pennies and nickels) was clamshell disks. These disks were made rather round and about the size of a nickel (called *so*). Clamshells were broken into pieces, then rounded and polished on a sandstone slab. The thicker the clamshell disks the better the Indians liked them.

The disks were strung like beads. A long string was worth

more than a short one. The clamshell money that was the oldest, or that had the best polish, had the most value. Money was measured by wrapping the string around the palm of the hand, the fingers, or the closed fist, once or twice or several times. A short string was measured just once around the hand and was worth very little. Some tribes stretched the string of clamshell money out straight and measured it that way.

Clamshell money.

The small, thin, white, tooth-like dentalium shells were hard to find and so worth much more than clamshell money. These shells were found along the northern coast for the most part but they were used in other parts of the state. Strings of dentalium were usually about twenty-seven and a half inches long. The string was measured much as we would measure cloth without a yardstick, by holding the string of shells from the thumb to the shoulder. The longer the string the more its worth, of course. If a man had several strings of dentalium money, he was thought to be very rich.

When white men first came to California they put certain values on strings of dentalium shells. A string of shells having eleven large dentaliums was worth about fifty dollars. If there were twelve smaller shells, the string was worth twenty dollars; if thirteen, it was worth ten dollars. This was real "Indian money" and as such was used in trade for many other things.

The small, olive-shaped olivella shells were used nearly everywhere in the state. In the north they were strung whole; in central and southern California, they were often broken up and rolled into thin disks. Neither kind had much value.

The haliotis shell, which is a form of abalone, was broken

into pieces and used in ornaments and necklaces. However, these shells were not used as money in most cases.

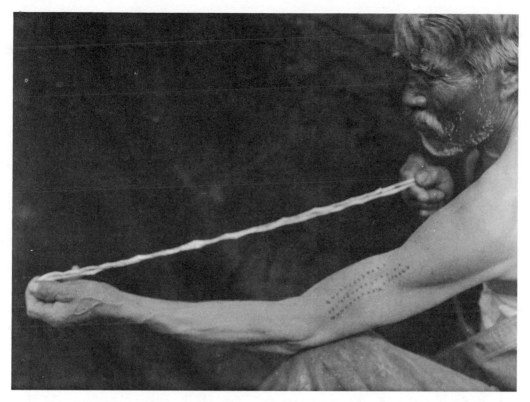

Strung dentalium shells were measured from the thumb to the shoulder. (Southwest Museum, Los Angeles)

The Pomo tribe took the hinges and curves of large clam-shells and polished them into long pieces. These were valuable ornaments but were not used except for trading. Some tribes found a kind of soft rock that we call magnesite. They rubbed or ground this into tubes about one to three inches long. They then baked the tubes until the heat turned them pink, red, or brown. As the magnesite tubes were worn they became shiny. These were worth more than shell money, just as gold is worth more to us than silver.

There were other uses for shells. Indians used all the beautiful shells they found for pendants, hairpins, necklaces, bracelets, and earrings. These were valuable in trade to inland tribes where there were no shells.

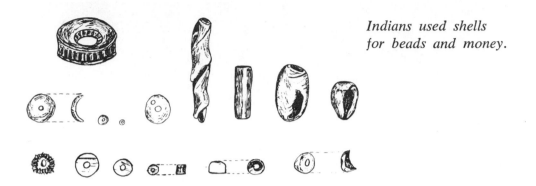

Indians used shells for beads and money.

A treasure worth almost as much as shell money was dried woodpecker scalps with soft red or green feathers. These were rare and since they were hard to get, they were valuable. The woodpecker scalps were traded for shell money or for any other wanted articles. Nothing was finer to wear to a dance or ceremony than a headband of red or green woodpecker scalps.

Deerskins that were either very light or very dark in color had great value. The common gray, light brown, or reddish brown skins were not worth much in trade. The Yurok tribe thought that white deerskin was worth so much it had to be kept in the family forever and used in ceremonial dances. All ceremonial clothes were cared for by the village chief and were greatly treasured.

Obsidian, the black volcanic glass, was worth about as much as dentalium or magnesite tubes. Red obsidian was very rare and was worth much more than the black. The longer the piece of obsidian, the more it was worth. Obsidian was used in some arrow points but it was more like a jewel to be worn and treasured. Large obsidian pieces were taken to dances and ceremonies and shown to visiting tribes. This proved that the owner was rich. Flint, a very hard stone, could be chipped very thin. It was worth a good deal also, especially if one had a long piece of it.

Men of the Wintun and Mohave tribes liked to travel and were good traders. They carried goods from tribe to tribe and their visits were usually welcomed. Other California Indians did not roam about much but each group kept in its own territory most of the time. However, they did trade back and forth with their nearest neighbors. Indians along the coast traded fish and shells to forest Indians for acorns and animal skins. The Pomo traded their beautifully made baskets for the things they wanted from other tribes nearby. The Hupa Indians in the mountains traded with their neighbors, the Yuroks, who lived along the

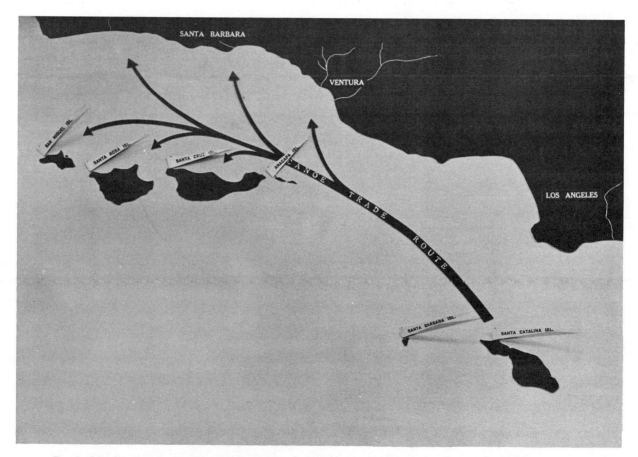

Probable trade route between island and mainland Indians. (Santa Barbara Museum of Natural History—Bosworth Lemere)

seashore. The Hupas gave seeds, nuts, and deerskins in return for redwood canoes, dried fish, and a salty seaweed they liked to eat. Indians near volcanic Mt. Lassen made obsidian tools and arrow points from volcanic glass and traded them to valley Indians for blankets and acorns.

One of the most useful materials that all tribes wanted and few had was the steatite or soapstone found chiefly on Santa Catalina Island. Small picks and sharp stones were used to shape steatite into fine cooking bowls and other things such as charmstones. Steatite was mined and brought to the mainland in canoes and traded for sandstone bowls, beads, and food, especially acorns. It is believed that the large steatite bowls were made on the island. Smaller articles were made on the mainland, many of them from pieces of cooking pots. Even the pieces of steatite were worth a good deal in trade.

So we see that Indians did not always use shell money to buy what they wanted. They traded by giving something they had for things from other tribes. Everything had its own value, just as it does today.

Steatite was shaped into bowls, pendants, pipes, charmstones, and many other articles. (Santa Barbara Museum of Natural History—Bosworth Lemere)

Chapter 12

CHIEFS AND MEDICINE MEN:
THEIR POWER AND MAGIC

Indians were usually an easygoing, free, and happy people. They had their own customs and rules and governed themselves quietly. No written laws were needed, no policemen or jails as we know them. People knew what they had to do. They knew that the chief of the village and the men of the council chosen by the people would see to it that their unwritten laws were obeyed. If people did not obey the rules, the chief and the council decided what had to be done. They were sometimes given a fine but most of the time the chief talked to them and told them that they had to get along with others and obey rules. This kind of government, by the chief, the council, and the people, kept peace in the village. One crime, however, was to take food given to the chief or headman that was supposed to be used by him when there were village feasts. If anyone dared to do this he might be killed. Rarely was there any fighting between villages or tribes unless food was taken without asking for it. A village or person that had a good supply had to protect it. Sometimes there were quarrels over acorn tree areas or fishing waters. Such quarrels were settled by the chiefs or headmen of the tribes. If there was fighting and anyone was killed, money was paid to the family of the person killed. The Yuma and Mohave were more war-like than other tribes and their chiefs were supposed to be very strong and brave.

Each band or village had a headman or chief. Usually he was made a chief because his father before him had been one. If he had no son, a brother or even his wife could be made the new chief. Sometimes the son was not a good man for a chief and then the people had to choose a chief. When the chief was chosen, it was because he had proved that he was an important man in the village. Perhaps he had more shell money than the others or perhaps a rare white deerskin. He was supposed to know more than the rest of the people. He settled quarrels much like a judge but he did not rule the people. One of his duties was to plan when and where ceremonies were to be held. It was he who invited visitors to join in celebrations. He gave food to the poorer villagers. Everyone in a village believed that he belonged to a big family and that his neighbors in the village should be helped in time of need. Those who had plenty shared food and gifts with the chief. People said, "He gives to all who need it. Let us help him because he works for all of us." When the chief had no more to give the village people gave him more. When he said, "Let us sing" or "Let us dance," the people gathered together and had a happy time. Villagers believed that their chiefs could do no wrong. The Chumash and the Juaneño were known to have fought against any group not friendly to their chiefs.

Besides the village chief or headman, there was a medicine man or *shaman*. The Indians believed what he told them because he not only knew magic but he knew about the many plants used for curing diseases.* The "rain doctor" said that he could make rain whenever it was needed. The "snake doctor" could handle rattlesnakes and cure snake bites, so he said. The "bear doctor" said that he had the power to turn himself into a grizzly bear. When changed into a bear, he could kill all his enemies. Most of the Indians did not know whether or not to believe him. They were not sure what he could do, so they feared him.

The Indian medicine man's powers began when he was young. At the time of drinking the Jimson weed (see Chapter 13), he may have had dreams of becoming a medicine man. When he thought that he was ready to become one, he invited the villagers to a special ceremony. He told them of his great power to cure diseases. He told them that pains and diseases were caused by objects that had to be "sucked out" or "blown out" of their bodies or removed by some other magic means. So the medicine man sucked or blew, spurted water, rubbed or waved feathers. Suddenly a live spider or a very sharp stone appeared in his hand. These were the things that had caused the pain, he said. How he did this trick was his secret.

The medicine man or *shaman* thought that he gained power by going without food for a long time or by taking drugs that caused dreams. Dreams of animals in the "other world" were supposed to tell him what to do. People thought that he could talk to both the "good spirits" and the "bad spirits." They showed respect to him because they did not want him to talk to the "bad spirits" about them. One thing that almost all

* See Addenda: "Some of the Important Plants Used for Medicine."

111

medicine men did know was the use of plants that cured diseases. When the medicine man cured the villagers everyone was happy. If he did not, he might be shot to death with arrows. Unlike other American Indian tribes the California Indians had medi-

It was believed that charmstones brought good luck. (Santa Barbara Museum of Natural History—Bosworth Lemere)

cine women as well as men. Medicine women were thought to have great power as doctors.

Some of the Chumash had another way of curing the sick or getting what they wanted. They placed twelve thin smooth stones in a circle and put some *chia* seeds in the middle. Over the *chia* they placed goose feathers and red dust. Three old men sat around the circle of stones and made strange noises. This kind of ceremony was supposed to cure the sick, bring rain, put out fires, bring fish, or help the tribe in case of war.

Charmstones of various shapes have been found that may have been "luck stones." It was believed that charmstones held over a stream would bring fish to the nets. Wild game would come toward the hunter if a charmstone was put on a rocky cliff. Arrows would not harm a warrior if he wore a charmstone about his neck.

A number of tribes, especially the Penutian family, had a secret society called *kuksu*. Usually their celebration was held in winter during the time of rain. After painting their faces white to look like "spirits," men met in a large earth-covered house. The head of the society was a very important man in a village. He took care of the people of his tribe in many ways. When he called men, both young and old, to a meeting, he dressed in a very large, round, feather headdress and some-

Shaman's *feather headdress.*

times a feather cape. While the men beat drums, he sang and danced and told the people about how the world was made and how the Indians came to be. His songs were like prayers as he told of the things he wished for his people—good health, good crops, and freedom from all harm. When the head of the *kuksu* society danced and chanted his songs, the older members and the new ones knew that he would tell them many things they needed to know about their tribe. It made them happy to hear that there was someone who made the world and who took care of them.

Chapter 13

OLD INDIAN BELIEFS

AND CUSTOMS

No one taught Indians about religion—where they came from
or where they were going. Even though it was a mystery, Indians
had their own ideas about such things. In the first place the
Indians had great respect for everything they found in nature.
To them the sun and the great redwood trees were very important. Some believed that in the beginning there was a Sky
father and an Earth mother. From these two came all things.
There were tribes who believed that the world was once a great
mass. Out of the mass a god made the world and put it on
the shoulders of seven giants. When one of the giants moved
there was an earthquake. After the world, the god made animals
and last of all he made man. Still others thought that animals

Indians had great respect for the giant redwood trees. (United States Forest Service)

made the world in the beginning. The Eagle was the maker and "good chief" of all. The Coyote with his sly ways was the "evil one." Both were respected, as was The Bear. The mountains and the streams had "spirits" in them, both good and bad, so they thought. Indians remembered these things when they wandered in the mountains or by rivers.

While there were those who thought there was one god, some believed in many gods. The one great god, so some believed, was *Chinigchinich*. If those in a village believed in him, an altar was built inside a round, mat-like fence. Eagle feathers and gifts of meal, tobacco, and arrows were offered to him on the altar. Sand paintings were carefully made by the altar as an offering also.

Sand paintings were made by the chief. (Southwest Museum, Los Angeles)

Indians did believe that there would be another life. The "other life" would be like this one except that there would be no trouble there. Everything they did in the "other life" would go well. Since the person would need things in the other world, some of his clothing, food, and treasures were buried (or burned) with him when he died.

Indians believed that the mountains and streams had "spirits" in them. (California Division of Forestry)

Indians did not exactly pray for what they wanted; they danced and sang about their needs. Many dances celebrated the coming of new seasons. They danced when they wanted luck in hunting, or to find something that would make them rich, or to be cured of an illness. When there was a new month, old men danced and sang, "As the moon dies and comes to life again, so we who die will live again." Chiefs, they believed, became stars in the sky and so they gave names to the stars.

Indians had many ceremonies even though they led simple lives. The age-old stories about the beliefs, customs, and ceremonies of Indian days have been passed down through the years. It is interesting to learn about some of these ceremonies that meant so much to the Indian people.

The Young Child

Soon after a child was born, it was tied to its cradle board. In this way the mother or an older child in the family could carry the baby about on her back. In cold weather a rabbit skin was thrown over the cradle to keep the baby warm. As the child grew older he ran about on sunny days with his mother. On foggy or cold days he stayed inside the house close to the fire. When he became six years old he was given a name. This was a time of celebration and village people met together for a "name-giving ceremony." The chief or headman held the child in his arms as he danced in a circle. As he did this, he gave the child the name. From that time on he was no longer thought of as a very young child.

Girls' Growing-Up Ceremony

When a girl reached the age of thirteen or fourteen, she was thought to be a grown-up person. Girls often married at the age of fifteen. When girls became that age, they were made to lie on a bed of hot sand for three or more days. This was sup-

Exhibit of Ceremonial Dress worn by the Pomo and Mohave tribes. (Santa Barbara Museum of Natural History—Bosworth Lemere)

posed to make them strong and good mothers some day. During this time, women danced around the girls, singing the old songs of the tribe. After this, the chief told the girls of the old beliefs of the tribe. He made a sand painting of the world on the ground. Looking at the sand picture, the girls thought about how the world was made. The chief told them that they were now old enough to be a part of the world. He made a lump of *chia* or sage seeds and salt and put it into the mouth of each girl. Each girl tasted the lump and dropped it into the sand picture. This was the way she made herself a part of the world. The picture was then swept away but the sage lumps were given back to the girls to keep among their treasures.

The Luiseño added to this custom by having the girls run a race to a rock near the village. Here the chief's wife painted designs on the girls' faces and put the same designs on the rock. Once a month, for four months, the girls were brought back to the rock. Each time a different design was used. After that they were thought to be true members of the Luiseño tribe.

A girl was tattooed on her chin just before she was married. All the Indians of the Pacific coast did this. They thought that the tattoos made girls more beautiful. It may not have made the girls beautiful but everyone could tell by the tattoos that they were married.

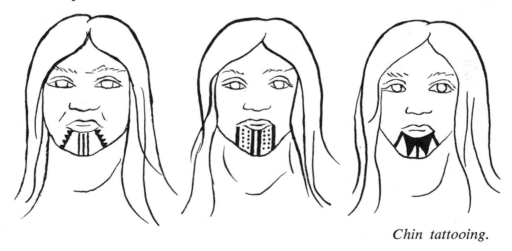

Chin tattooing.

Boys' Growing-Up Ceremony

Boys had to go through even more than girls when they became fourteen or fifteen. Since they had to be strong in later years, they had to prepare for the future. Old Indians believed that magic to make young men strong came from a plant known to them as *tololache*. To us it is known as Jimson weed, a plant with huge white bell-like flowers. The root of the plant was chopped fine and mixed with water. All who drank of the mixture had dreams. It would kill anyone who drank very much of it. Older Indians watched to see that the young men drank just enough and no more.

A coming-of-age ceremony for boys was held by almost all the tribes. Men from nearby villages brought their young boys and came to help in the ceremony. A brush fence was built in a large circle just outside the village. The men brought the boys to the center of this circle. The leader of the visiting tribe mixed the drink. Each boy took some of the bitter water. Then the men led them back into the village where the village people waited to greet them. A fire was built and as the men hummed and danced around the fire, the boys became sleepy. When they did, the men took them back to the circle outside the village. Here the boys were left to have their dreams. Perhaps some dreamed of hunting and killing a wild animal. Others may have dreamed of taking long journeys without getting tired. Words or songs may have come to them in their dreams that made them feel brave. Whatever the dream, it was believed that some day he would be able to do or to become what he had dreamed about.

After the dreams were over the older men came back. Boys told them about their wonderful dreams. Then the men sang to them and told them things they thought they should know. Some of the things they may have told the boys were: "The earth helps you. The sky sees what you do. Everyone will see that you are good if you do right. Right will always win out over wrong and good will always win out over evil. Believe these things. Tell them to your sons later. If you do, you will live long." These were the lessons taught to the young boys by the men of the tribe.

Then the men made sand paintings much like those made for the girls' ceremony. Boys chewed sage balls and dropped them into the sand painting. In this way they, too, became a part of the tribe and the world. The sand was swept away but the sage balls were taken by the men to a hiding place and left there. The men said that the boys had now become men. They were ready to go hunting and fishing for the family's food.

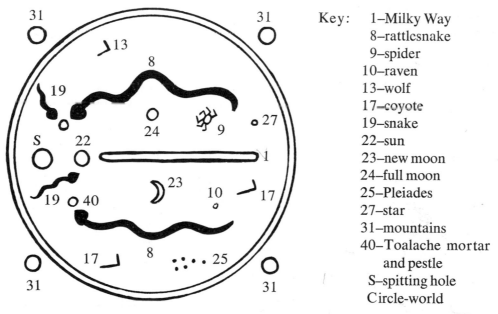

Key:
1–Milky Way
8–rattlesnake
9–spider
10–raven
13–wolf
17–coyote
19–snake
22–sun
23–new moon
24–full moon
25–Pleiades
27–star
31–mountains
40–Toalache mortar
   and pestle
S–spitting hole
Circle–world

A sand painting was made at both the boys' and the girls' growing-up ceremonies.

The final test of manhood came when the boys were eighteen. After a night of dancing, the chief and older men took the young men outside the village. Lessons were taught to them about rules of the tribe and about the work that they would have to do later. Not all tribes had the same kind of tests but all a young man had to do was to prove that he would be brave. And so the customs of these people passed from one generation to another.

Marriage

When he was ready to marry, the young man looked around for a girl who was good at gathering acorns and making baskets. She did not have to be beautiful. The important thing was that the Indian did not want a lazy wife. She was not usually from his own village but, as a rule, was from his tribe. Robes of squirrel or deerskin, arrow points, skin, or strings of beads were given to the bride's parents as gifts. The young man who gave the most gifts was almost always able to get the girl he wanted for his wife. If he did not have many gifts, he gave what he had and went to live with the bride's parents to work for them. In this way he showed the parents that he was a good worker and able to care for their daughter.

The marriage ceremony was a simple one. The medicine

Miwok dance headdress.

Yuki dance headdress.

man decorated the girl with the finest feathers he had. Dancers circled around her as they sang and told her that she must work hard, and be honest and kind. After the villagers had danced and feasted, the ceremony was over.

Death

An important ceremony was held when anyone in the tribe died. Neighboring tribes were invited to come. Although some tribes buried their dead, many burned them. The house and part of the person's belongings were burned at the same time.

Certain tribes believed that a widow should shorten her hair by cutting or burning. Northern California women wore a mourning necklace for a year. Some made belts from the hair that had been cut off.

The real mourning ceremony came about a year later. Before the ceremony little images were made out of grasses or cattails. Great care was used in making and dressing the statues. On the back of each one was put a little net with meal or a gift in it. These were for the journey to the "other world." At the ceremony songs were sung all night and there was feasting in the morning. As everyone sang, the family threw the images one by one into the fire. While this was going on there was singing, chanting, and mourning. After the ceremony was over, the dead person's name was never spoken of again although he was never forgotten.

Eagle Ceremony

Another important ceremony was given in honor of the eagle. The eagle's feathers were much respected, because they were used for ceremonial clothes. There were those who believed that the eagle existed before man and that therefore eagle feathers had a certain magic. They thought that once the eagle had flown north, south, east, and west. When he could not escape, he was willing to have people use his feathers for special occasions.

Eagles' nests were very valuable to a tribe and they were guarded closely. A chief would take the young eagles from the nests and keep them in his home. After the eagle was older, the feathers were ready to be plucked at a special ceremony. The chief called the people together and told them that it was time to send the eagle to the "other world." He said to the people, "Here is a messenger ready to go to the 'other world.' Do you have any messages to go—either good or evil?" There

Dance headband worn by the Pomo.

was great mumbling among the people as they told their messages to the eagle. As the medicine man looked at the eagle with his piercing eyes, the eagle fell dead. Perhaps he choked the eagle but the people believed that it was his magic. The eagle's feathers were taken to be made into ceremonial skirts later. As for the eagle, he was cast into the fire so that he could go to the "other world" with the messages. Then men put on their eagle skirts and danced wildly in a circle. As they did, the feathers spread out wide around them and seemed to soar as the eagle had once done.

The Swordfish Dance

Chumash Indians thought that the swordfish was a very special friend of their tribe. They were certain that it was the swordfish that drove whales to the shore where they could be caught for food. Whenever a whale washed up on the beach, the village people had plenty to eat for weeks. The Chumash had a swordfish dance in which they wore a scaly headdress that looked like the head of the swordfish (such a headdress has been found in a Chumash grave). As the Indians danced they gave thanks to the swordfish for his kindness. They probably asked that more whales be sent to the shore!

Exhibit showing Swordfish Ceremony. (Santa Barbara Museum of Natural History—Bosworth Lemere)

Chapter 14

ONCE UPON A TIME

INDIAN TALES

Indians had many stories about the world in which they lived and the other "spirit world." Their stories told of the eagle, so important, and the coyote, so clever and cunning. They wanted so much to know how the world was made, about thunder and lightning, earthquakes and everything else around them. Because they could not understand all these things they made up stories about them. These stories were told from father to son and from one tribe to another until at last they seemed to be true.

How Man Was Made
One of the tales was about the Coyote, who wished to make men on earth. All the animals were called together so the Coyote

could get their advice as to how this could be done. "Let man have a voice that can roar and sharp teeth and claws. Then he can scare other animals," said the Lion. Grizzly Bear did not agree. He thought it much more important that man be very strong. Deer thought that man should have beautiful round horns. Mountain Sheep said that if he had straight horns they would get caught in the bushes. "His horns should be rolled up like mine," said the Mountain Sheep. The Owl thought that man should have wings and the Mouse thought he should have sharp eyes so that he could see what he was eating.

Coyote listened to what they told him. "All of you are foolish animals for all of you want man to be like yourselves. Man should be all of the things you say but he should be as wise as I am!" Thus spoke the Coyote.

Finally, the animals set to work to make man out of lumps of clay. Each worked to make man look like himself until each one grew so tired that he fell asleep. The wise old Coyote stayed awake and decided that he would fool the other animals. While they were asleep he threw water on their clay until it melted away. By morning when the animals awakened, the Coyote had made man. He made him just the way that he thought he should be—the best part of each of the animals. Thus man was made by the Coyote.

YOKUTS LEGEND

How Fire and Light Came to the New Land

After the people and the land were made, Mr. Lizard found it to be a cold and dark place. There was no light; no fire to make him warm. So he sent his friend, little white-footed Mouse, to a faraway land to steal fire. The Mouse stole the fire and hurried away with it as fast as he could. Just then he heard someone running after him. He hid his bright spark of fire in the cedar and buckeye trees nearby. Suddenly there was a great burst of fire in the trees. It seemed to blaze up as high

Suddenly a great fire blazed up. (United States Forest Service)

as the sky! From this came the sun—warm and bright—and in this way light came to the New Land.

Not all the trees caught on fire and flamed so high. Some of the fire was so covered with branches that it only smoked. Since then, men have been able to rub twigs together and the fire comes to life all over again.

Story of El Capitan in Yosemite Valley

Many long years ago two little boys went out to play in a grassy valley (which the Indians call *Ahwahnee*). They splashed and swam in the stream that ran through the valley until they were tired out. Then they climbed onto a large rock and fell asleep. No sooner had they done so than the rock on which they were lying began to grow. In those days the Indians thought that rocks did this. The rock grew higher and higher—up and up—until it seemed to touch the sky. Still the boys slept on.

The rock that grew and grew—El Capitan, Yosemite National Park. (Hubert A. Lowman)

Their mother called to her children but there was no answer. She called the animals together and asked them to help her find the boys. The animals told her about the children on the rock and what must have happened. All of them wondered how they could get the boys down. One by one each animal tried to climb up the face of the rock but failed. About that time along came a little measuring worm. He was the kind of worm that traveled very slowly but very surely. The animals asked him if he would crawl up the big rock and he said that he would try. Slowly, ever so slowly, inch by inch, he edged up and up and up! Soon the tiny worm was so high that no one could see him any more.

The mother and the animals waited for a very long time at the foot of the mighty cliff that was nearly a mile high. They did not know it but the little worm had not given up. At last he reached the top of the stony cliff where the boys were sleeping. The measuring worm awakened them and slowly brought them safely down to their mother.

In later years, this huge rocky cliff was given the name El Capitan.

How the People Learned

The New People made by Coyote found that the land was fair and that there was plenty of food. Men learned to live by watching to see how the animals lived. They went into the woods and found food that was good to eat. From the Crane they learned to spear and eat fish. From Trout they learned how to swim. Deer taught the New People how to run fast. Ants taught them that much could be done by working together. Birds, with their happy songs, taught the New People that there was joy in the world. Indian women watched the birds build their nests, and from this they learned how to weave baskets.

From all the creatures, great and small, the people learned

how to live in the New Land. They grew in numbers and became strong. The people looked at the Sun and gave thanks for its light and warmth and for making things grow. They danced to give thanks to the One who had made them and the world they lived in.

An Indian storage basket for piñon nuts made like a bird's nest. (Hubert A. Lowman)

Chapter 15

WHAT BECAME OF THE INDIANS?

We learned in the beginning about the first explorers who came to California and brought back reports of seeing Indians living along the coast. Each time the explorers came, the Indians must have wondered why they came and what would happen next. As we found out, there were no explorers for over a hundred and sixty years. Indians kept on living in the same ways they had always known.

Then there was interest in California all over again. Russian ships landed on the north coast of America. There they found otters and seals, the skins of which could be sold to make fine, warm coats. People of cold countries were glad to pay high prices for such furs. The Russians kept coming nearer and nearer to California. News about this went back to Spain. Spain had also heard about other countries that had become interested in California. Now Spain saw that something had to be done quickly to keep land once claimed for her by the early Spanish explorers.

It was decided that the time had come for action. Spain knew that someone should be chosen to go to California who knew something about the Indian people who were living there. At the time, Father Junípero Serra was president of the Lower (Baja) California missions. As such, he had worked with and taught the Indians there. Years before he had heard of California and had wanted to go there. He was delighted when told that he had been chosen to live and work among the Indians there.

Gaspar de Portolá, the Spanish governor of Lower (Baja) California, was told to head a party of soldiers into California. The plan was to build *presidios* or forts along the coast where soldiers could live. The soldiers were to protect Spain's right to California and drive out explorers from other countries who dared to claim it.

After the *presidios,* Father Serra was to direct the building of missions. Each mission was to have not only a chapel for worship but also workshops, rooms for visitors, and small homes where the Indians could live. Indian families were to leave their own homes, help build the missions, live and work there. They were to help the padres in any useful way: grow crops for food, make articles needed at the mission, and also to learn about the Christian religion. It was expected that someday the mission chapel would become the church in a town or *pueblo* that would grow up around it. It was thought that by this time the Indians would be given the mission lands and they could then build their homes and in every way care for themselves.

Fifty-four years passed by (1769–1823). Four *presidios* were built at San Diego, Santa Barbara, Monterey and San Francisco. Twenty-one missions were built during that period from the south to the north of the state.* Indians were brought to missions where they built their little homes and had a new kind of life. All who came were promised a better way of life and plenty of food. However, there was much hard work to be done and the Indians did it, even though it was different from any work done before. Thousands of adobe bricks and tiles were made by Indian hands. They learned to make useful things in the mission workshops; they grew crops and built irrigation ditches to bring water to the missions and the gardens. Women did the cooking, weaving, caring for children and helped in many ways. Life was secure but was this what the Indians really wanted? They had been used to a free life. How hard it must have been for them to stay in one place when they had been used to roaming, to be farmers instead of food-gatherers and hunters. So many kinds of work and living had to be learned.

Thousands of Indians died from diseases for which they knew no cure.** It was hard to learn a new language (Spanish) and to understand the new Christian story told by the padres. Many were content but some ran away from the missions. When they were brought back by the soldiers they were punished. It is easy to understand why these were such difficult years for the Indians. Padres also had to do work for which they had not been trained. Not only did they teach about religion but they taught how to build, make things in the workshops such as furniture and saddles, grow crops and raise cattle; and they had to act as innkeepers for visitors who came and in all ways direct the work of the missions. As time went on the mission lands grew larger and richer.

Another change came on April 11, 1822, when the flag of the Mexican Empire was raised at the Monterey *presidio*. News soon

See Bauer, California Mission Days.
*** See Addenda: "Plants Used for Medicine."*

136

Adobe bricks made by Indians were used to build mission walls. (Arthur Barr Productions, Inc.) From Bauer, California Mission Days.

spread that California no longer belonged to Spain but to Mexico. In 1834 word came from Mexico that the missions were no longer needed and were to be closed. Padres gradually left the missions and went to live in Spain and Mexico from which they had come and to Mission Santa Barbara (Santa Barbara). Part of the land was given to the Indians as planned. However, now there was no one to help them in their new way of life or to protect them from outsiders. It was not long before their lands were either sold for a little money, perhaps traded away for a few horses or blankets, or, as in most cases, just taken away from them. Missions gradually fell into ruins or were damaged by earthquakes. New ways had been only partly learned and with their lands gone there was little left for them to do but to return to their old ways in places they knew best.

Mexican settlers and newcomers began to build little adobe houses and grow crops on what was once mission and Indian lands. Such lands were broken up into *ranchos,* and *rancheros* became the new owners. This was the beginning of a new period in California's history.* Indians who knew how to farm or raise cattle were taken to work on the *ranchos.* Indian women were also taken to live on *ranchos* where they helped with the cooking, the care of children, and many kinds of useful work. For many years, former mission Indians did all the hard work on the *ranchos.* When they grew tired of this kind of life, they joined their friends and relatives who lived in the mountains and valleys.

Other changes were ahead for the Indians and all Californians. Mexico and the United States both wanted California and they fought a war to get it. On January 13, 1847, a paper was signed by United States Colonel John C. Frémont and Mexican General Andrés Pico. This paper was the Treaty of Guadalupe Hidalgo. Under this treaty, the United States agreed that Indians had a right to land on which they lived.** California's part in the Mexican War was over and one year later, in February 1848, the United States made final peace with Mexico. It was not until September 1850 that California became the thirty-first state in the United States.

When all this was happening, gold was found at Coloma on the South Fork of the American River. Thousands of people

---

* *See Bauer,* California Rancho Days.
** *Indians lived on eighty-four million acres of land at the time of the Treaty of Guadalupe Hidalgo (1853) but the agreement of this treaty was not kept. It was not until 1965 that a settlement was made. The Indians Claims Commission granted $29.1 million dollars for the land to Indians who could trace their ancestry back to an Indian living in 1853, the time when the land was taken away from the Indians.*

Indians went to work on the ranchos. (*Arthur Barr Productions, Inc.*) *From Bauer,* California Rancho Days.

flocked to California by land and sea from all over the United States and the world.* These were important years in the history of California and the world but were very sad ones for the Indians. They could not understand the mad scramble for the shiny gold. What use did it have? Neither could they understand why the gold-seekers cut down so many trees, why they muddied the beautiful streams. Indians had always loved nature; it was part of their religion. They had always taken from nature what was needed, nothing more. Never before had they seen gold-hungry and land-hungry men pound stakes into the ground and

* *See Bauer,* California Gold Days.

say, "This piece of earth is mine!" Was not *all* the land in California *their* land? After they realized what was happening it was too late. Oak trees that had once given them acorns for food were cut down; fish were driven from the streams and animals were driven far back into the mountains. Many Indians fell ill and died from diseases brought by the white men and from lack of food. Indians fought to keep the new settlers off their land but there were too many of them and they had guns ("thunder sticks" they called them). Where towns sprang up there was no room for Indians. Even in places where miners did not go, small groups of Indians stayed for a while and then moved on. By this time they were very poor and not able to take care of themselves with what they had left. Once they had been an honest and peaceful people. Now some of them began to steal food, horses and supplies from the gold-seekers. As a result they were hunted down and shot. So year after year, the number of Indians grew less and less.*

Nothing was done to protect the Indians until the 1850s. The United States sent government people to make treaties with the Indians. Eighteen treaties were made but less than half of the Indians of the state were included. The treaties provided that Indians were to give up their claims to California lands. In return they were to receive eight and a half million acres of land and such things as food, clothing, and tools and schools would be built for their children. This might have been a good way to help provide for some of their needs but years went by and the United States did not sign the treaties. It was fifty years later before the Indians found that they had no treaty rights. In 1851 the United States government set up a commission to decide on lands claimed by all former mission Indians (as given in the Treaty of Guadalupe Hidalgo in 1847). Indians were not told about this and if they had been, might not have known how to

* *Before the white man came there were about 150,000 California Indians. By 1890 only about 17,000 of them were left and many of them were of mixed blood.*

Present-day reservation Indian boy beside rock where acorns were once pounded into meal. (Hubert A. Lowman)

go about making claims for the land. So the land was taken away and given to the government.

Year after year the Indians lost more and more of their land. Finally (1850–1860), the United States government set aside certain lands for them called reservations. The idea seemed to be to get Indians out of the white man's way, to put them in a place where they would be protected. The government became the guardian (or caretaker) and Indians became what was called "wards" (or those who receive care). This did not mean that the government had a right to control each Indian as a person. It did mean that the government had control over the reservation land, its sale and its use (even as they do today).*

Through the years hundreds of treaties have been made with Indian tribes in America. Some have been kept but most of them have not. Rules have been changed many times. Today, reservation Indians have their important tribal councils. They make their own plans and they work with the government to make plans that will be best for their people. There are many problems but most of the Indians do not want to give up reservation land. This land is home to them and they wish to keep it. They know their needs and more and more they are speaking out as *one people* to tell about them. They would like just enough help to help themselves and no more. Indians want for their families the same things that all Americans do—good jobs, homes, schools and good health conditions.

Most reservation homes are very poor and better homes are needed. There is a very high rate of diseases among Indians. Better health conditions are needed and more people who can help to make this possible. More and better schools are needed; more Indian teachers. As it is, few Indian students finish high school, and few get a college education. Money is needed to send more young people to college. If they get a good education, they can become the leaders of their people in the years ahead. More Indians should be trained for various kinds of work. Small factories could be built by and owned by reservation Indians (and this is being done in some places).

What of the thousands of Indians who have left reservations and gone to live in cities? There are about thirty thousand living

* As of July 1967, there were seventy-three reservations and rancherías in California. Some of them are very small (from two to twenty-five thousand acres). The largest reservation is the Hoopa Valley Reservation in northern California (Humboldt County). Over nine hundred Indians live there along the Trinity River.

in the Los Angeles area and about twenty thousand in the San Francisco area. They have left their homes on reservations and found a new kind of life in cities and towns. At first, the life in any city is very difficult. The Indian is afraid, just as anyone else would be or even more so. Everything is strange to him, life is very different—and very fast. He must learn to live with people he does not know; find a home in which to live and the kind of work he can do. He may receive some help from others but much depends on himself. In time, he is usually able to become a part of the life around him. Many Indians work in offices, factories, and trades of all kinds. Some are engineers, businessmen, writers, and teachers. Whatever work they do and wherever they live, they continue to think of themselves as Indians. They can think of the past and take pride in it. When they wish to go back to the reservation to visit or to live, they may do so.

Today, some parts of the very old Indian culture remain. Each generation seems to know a little less about the old ways. There are those who still remember songs, stories, and customs told to them as children. Few women weave the beautiful baskets anymore. Materials are hard to find and it is not easy to make such baskets. Some of the older men remember the very old ceremonies and still take part in them on the reservations. Indians still dance the old dances, not only on reservations but in public places on special occasions. This is one part of Indian culture that the tourists see. The graceful, rhythmic dances and the colorful costumes are enjoyed by all who see them. Even though dances may not have the old-time meaning, it is said that the Indian dancer finds that such dancing is still one way of feeling he is an Indian and he finds great joy in it.

Indians still have special celebrations every year. There is one celebration, for example, at Pala (San Diego County, near Mount Palomar where a giant telescope is located). Here there is Mission San Antonio de Pala, which was built by Luiseño

The church at Pala, built by the Luiseños, is the only church left from mission days which is still attended by Indians. (Hubert A. Lowman)

Indians during mission days. Indians still go to services in the church and each year they have a special day of celebration. People march with banners and lighted torches. A dinner is served to friends and visitors and there are games and a program of Indian and Mexican songs and dances.

In the very earliest times, Indians, who were our first Americans, crossed over a sea or land bridge into the New World (see Chapter 1). In modern times, there is another bridge that they have crossed, from old to new ways. The Indian well knows his past; he knows that he has come a long way and that it has been very hard. Much of what has happened to Indians in the past should not have happened. However, today more and more people are watching out for the Indian's interests and needs and are trying to do something about them.* The Indian may say, "I know where I have been. Where am I going?" The way ahead is still not certain. One important thing he does know he is proud to be an Indian. His past should not be forgotten by any American for it is a very important part of the history of our country as well as of California. Indians should be given every chance to look back to their past with pride and to their future with hope that the years ahead will be better ones for them.

---

* In February 1968 President Lyndon B. Johnson asked Congress for a half million dollars to improve the lot of six hundred thousand American Indians. He asked for such things as: six hundred new aides for a health program; for a thousand new houses to be built for them each year; for more job opportunities and better training; for more teachers in Indian schools and for more money to send Indians to college. A National Council on Indian Opportunity has been set up to push ahead these plans and make them possible.

Addenda

IN WHAT FORMER INDIAN TERRITORY
DO YOU LIVE TODAY?

In most cases the Indian villages were not located within the boundaries of present-day cities or else there were many small villages clustered in or around the sites of present California cities.

INDIAN VILLAGES WERE LOCATED ON THE SAME SITE OF (OR NEAR) THESE PRESENT CITIES

PRESENT CITY	INDIAN VILLAGE OR VILLAGES	PRESENT CITY	INDIAN VILLAGE OR VILLAGES
Auburn	Hangwite	Petaluma	Meleya
Azusa	Asuksa	Piru	Pi'idhuku
Bakersfield	Woilo	Placerville	Poktono, Pota
Calistoga	Nigletk-sonoma	Pomona	Toibi
Carpinteria	Michopshdo	Porterville	Chokowisho, Koyeti
Chico	Kolok		
Colfax	Umucha	Redondo Beach	Engva
Colton	Takema	Sacramento	Sutamasina
	Wacha-Vak	St. Helena	Anakotanoma
Escondido	Mehelom-Pom-Pauvo	Salinas	Saho-n
		San Bernardino	Kotaina
Fort Ross	Meteni	San Diego	Pu-shuyi
Fresno	Wakichi	San Fernando	Pasek
Gaviota	Mich'lyu	San Francisco	Awas-te
Goleta	Heliok, Paltocac	San Gabriel	Siba
Grass Valley	Tipotoya	San Jose	Wermerse-n
Hollister	Mutsun	San Mateo	Matala-n
Hueneme	Weneme	San Miguel	Teshaya
Jackson	Tukupe-su	San Pedro	Masau
Knights Landing	Vodol	San Rafael	Awani-wi
Lakeport	Kashibadon	Santa Barbara	Siuhtun, Alpincha
Lompoc	Lompoc	Santa Clara	Tamia-n
Long Beach	Shua	Santa Cruz	Sokel
Los Alamos	Masuwuk	Santa Maria	Nipomo
Los Angeles	Wenot, Yangna	Santa Monica	Saa-n
Mariposa	Kasumati	Santa Paula	Mupu
Martinez	Saklan	Saticoy	Satikoi
Marysville	Humata	Saugus	Liwanelowa
Mendocino	Buldam	Sebastopol	Batiklechawi
Mesa Grande	Tukumak	Sespe	Sekspe
Monterey	Tamo-tk	Simi	Shimyli
Monticello	Topaidi-hi	Sonoma	Huchi
Mugu, Point	Wihachet	Sonora	Kuluti
Napa	Tulukai	Temecula	Temaku
Novato	Chokeche	Ventura	Shisholop
Ojai	Ahwat	Visalia	Yokodo
Oroville	Apautawilu	Yosemite	Awani
Paso Robles	Cholame	Yountville	Kalmus

CALIFORNIA PLACE NAMES LEFT BY THE INDIANS

The Indians left their place names scattered thickly over the map of California; names of counties, cities, mountains, rivers, and valleys. Californians are apt to take place names for granted but the names had meanings to those of other days. We know that California has many Spanish place names and we understand many of them. We are not apt to know Indian names when we see them. Even when we do, we do not usually know what the name means. Much of this part of our history has been lost.

There are nine counties in the state that have Indian names: Colusa, Modoc, Mono, Napa, Shasta, Tehama, Tuolumne, Yolo, and Yuba. Two others, Inyo and Siskiyou, are supposed to be Indian. We do not know the meanings of any of the above names. We know that Indians usually did not use the names of people for places. Words they used were usually about something that happened or the place where it happened, such as "clover valley," "red rock," "snow mountains," or "bear place." Check the names below and perhaps you will find Indian place names in the area where you live.

NAME	MEANING	COUNTY
Aguanga	Luiseño village name	Riverside
Ahwahnee	Miwok village in Yosemite Valley	Madera
Anacapa (Island)	Chumash name	Ventura
Azusa	Gabrielino, "skunk place"	Los Angeles
Cabazon	Cahuilla Indian chief	Riverside
Cahuenga (Pass)	Gabrielino village name	Los Angeles
Cajalco	Cahuilla, "gathering place of waters"	Riverside
Calabasas	Chumash, "place of wild goose"	Los Angeles
Calpella	Indian chief (culpalan), "shellfish bearer"	Mendocino
Camulos	Chumash, "a fruit"	Ventura
Carquinez (Strait)	Wintun village	Contra Costa
Castaic	Shoshonean, "our eyes"	Los Angeles
Chemehuevi (Mts.)	Name of tribe	San Bernardino
Cholame	Salinan Indian village	San Luis Obispo
Chowchilla	Yokut, "murderers"	Madera
Coahuila	Probably Cahuilla tribe	Riverside
Coalinga	"place of coal"	Fresno
Cohasset	Algonkian, Koowas—"pines" and "it" or "pines place"	Butte
Coloma	Maidu village	El Dorado
Colusa	Wintun village	Colusa
Cucamonga	Shoshonean place name	San Bernardino
Cuyamaca	"rain yonder"	San Diego
Gualala	Pomo, "meeting place of waters"	Mendocino
Hemet	Luiseño, "corn valley"	Riverside
Hetch-Hetchy (Valley)	Miwok, name of plant that bears edible seed	Tuolumne
Hoopa (Hupa)	Yurok, Indian name of the valley	Humboldt
Hueneme	Chumash, "place of security"	Ventura

NAME	MEANING	COUNTY
Inyo (County)	Shoshonean, an Indian tribe	Inyo
Jacumba	Diegueño, "hut by the water"	San Diego
Jalama	Name of Chumash village, meaning unknown	Santa Barbara
Jamacao	Diegueño, "wild squash plant"	San Diego
Jamul	Diegueño, "foam"	San Diego
Jolon	Salinan village	Monterey
Kaweah	Yokut word, meaning unknown	Tulare
Klamath	Klamath name, perhaps "people"	Del Norte
Lompoc	Chumash, "little lake" or "little lagoon"	Santa Barbara
Malibu	Chumash village, "Maliwu"	Los Angeles
Marin (County)	Probably Spanish word for Coast Miwok headman	Marin
Matilija	Chumash village name	Ventura
Modoc (County)	Lutuami name for "south"	Modoc
Mojave	Mohave name for their tribe	Kern
Mokelumne Hill	Miwok village, name said to mean "people of Mokel"	Calaveras
Mono (County)	Yokut name for branch of Shoshoneans	Mono
Morongo (Valley)	"serrano," "meadow"	San Bernardino
Mugu (Point)	Chumash, "beach"	Ventura
Napa	Pomo name for "harpoon point"	Napa
Natoma	Maidu, "upstream"	Sacramento
Nipomo	Chumash village	San Luis Obispo

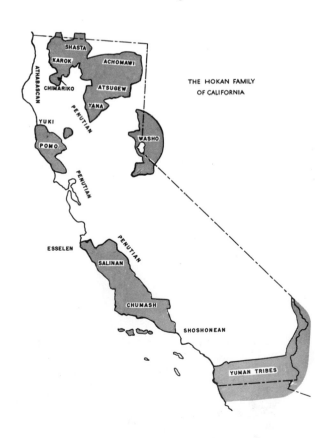

THE HOKAN FAMILY OF CALIFORNIA

NAME	MEANING	COUNTY
Noyo	Pomo village name, meaning unknown	Mendocino
Ojai	Chumash, "moon"	Ventura
Olancha	Yokut tribe or village	Inyo
Pacoima	Gabrielino place name	Los Angeles
Pala	Luiseño, "water"	San Diego
Petaluma	Coast Miwok, "flat-back"	Sonoma
Piru	Shoshonean name of a Chumash village, "plant" or "grass"	Ventura
Pismo Beach	Chumash name	San Luis Obispo
Piute	Shoshonean, "water Ute"	San Bernardino
Poway	Luiseño, "meeting of the valleys"	San Diego
Saticoy	Chumash village	Ventura
Sespe	Chumash village name, said to mean "fish"	Ventura
Shasta (City)	Name of Shasta headman?	Shasta
Simi	Chumash place name	Ventura
Siskiyou (County)	Indian word, meaning unknown	Siskiyou
Sisquoc	Chumash village name, meaning unknown	Santa Barbara
Soboba (Hot Springs)	Indian village name, meaning unknown	Riverside
Somis	Chumash village name	Ventura

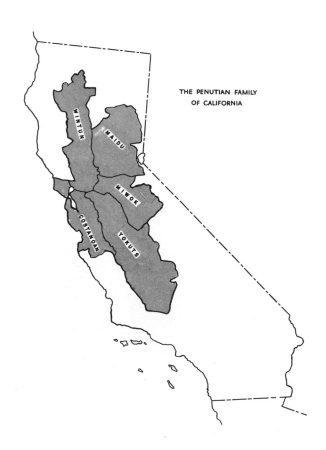

THE PENUTIAN FAMILY
OF CALIFORNIA

NAME	MEANING	COUNTY
Sonoma	Wappo word, "village of"	Sonoma
Stanislaus (County)	Chief of Consumnes or "earth village"	Stanislaus
Suisun	Wintun village name	Solano
Tahoe (City)	Washo, "big water" (Taa-oo)	Placer
Tamalpais (Mt.)	Coast Miwok, "bay mountain"	Marin
Tehachapi	Shoshonean, "land of acorns"	Kern
Tehama	Wintun village	Tehama
Temecula	Luiseño, "sun"	Riverside
Tomales (Bay)	Coast Miwok, "bay" (tamal)	Marin
Topanga	Gabrielino place name	Los Angeles
Topock	Mohave, "bridge"	San Bernardino
Tuolumne (County)	Miwok or Yokut (unknown)	Tuolumne
Tujunga	Gabrielino village	Los Angeles
Ukiah	Pomo, "south valley"	Mendocino
Weott	Wyot place name	Humboldt
Yolo	South Wintun, "place of the rushes"	Yolo
Yosemite	Indian village, "grizzly bear" perhaps	Mariposa
Yreka	Indian name for Mount Shasta (I-e-ka)	Siskiyou
Yuba	Yuba, meaning unknown	Yuba
Yucaipa	Shoshonean village name	San Bernardino

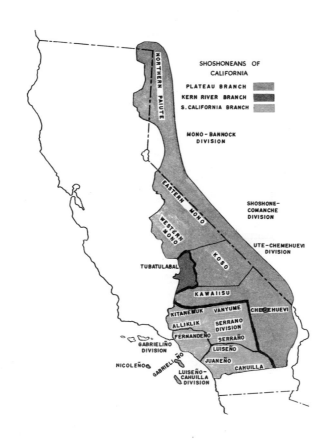

153

RESERVATIONS AND RANCHERÍAS IN CALIFORNIA*

RESERVATION OR RANCHERÍA	TRIBE	NEAREST TOWN
Agua Caliente Reservation	Coahuila	Palm Springs, California
* Also Cahuilla	or Cahuilla	
Alturas Ranchería	Pit River	Alturas, California
Augustine Reservation	Coahuila	Thermal, California
	or Cahuilla	
Barona Reservation	Diegueño	Alpine, California
Baron Long Reservation	Diegueño	Lakeside, California
(also known as Viejas		
Reservation)		
Berry Creek Ranchería	—	Berry Creek, California
Big Bend Ranchería	Pit River	Big Bend, California
Big Lagoon Ranchería	—	Orick, California
Big Pine Reservation	Paiute	Big Pine, California
Bishop Reservation	Paiute	Bishop, California
Cabazon Reservation	Coahuila	Indio, California
	or Cahuilla	
Cahuilla Reservation	Coahuila	Anza, California
	or Cahuilla	
Campo Reservation	Diegueño	Campo, California
Capitan Grande Reservation	—	Lakeside, California
Cedarville Ranchería	Paiute	Cedarville, California
Colusa Ranchería	Wintun	Colusa, California
(also known as Cachil Dehe)		
Cortina Ranchería	Mewuk	Williams, California
Cosmit Reservation	Diegueño	Julian, California
Cuyapaipe Reservation	Diegueño	Pine Valley, California
Dry Creek Ranchería	Pomo	Geyserville, California
Enterprise Ranchería	Maidu	Oroville, California
Fort Bidwell Reservation	Paiute	Fort Bidwell, California
Fort Independence Reservation	Paiute	Independence, California
Grindstone Creek Ranchería	Wintun	Orland, California
Hoopa Reservation	Hoopa	Hoopa, California
Hoopa Extension Reservation	Yurok	Weitchpec, California
Inaja Reservation	Diegueño	Julian, California
Jackson Ranchería	Mewuk	Jackson, California
LaJolla Reservation	Luiseño	Valley Center, California
La Posta Reservation	Luiseño	Boulevard, California
Laytonville Ranchería	Cahto	Laytonville, California
Lone Pine Reservation	Shoshone	Lone Pine, California
	& Paiute	
Lookout Ranchería	Pit River	Lookout, California
Los Coyotes Reservation	Luiseño	Warner Springs, California
Manchester-Pt. Arena Ranchería	Pomo	Point Arena, California
Manzanita Reservation	Diegueño	Pine Valley, California
Mesa Grande Reservation	Luiseño	Santa Ysabel, California
Middletown Ranchería	Pomo	Middletown, California

* Department of the Interior, Bureau of Indian Affairs, Sacramento, California.

RESERVATION OR RANCHERÍA	TRIBE	NEAREST TOWN
Mission Creek Reservation	Serrano	White Water, California
Montgomery Creek Ranchería	Pit River	Montgomery Creek, California
Morongo Reservation	Serrano	Banning, California
Pala Reservation	Luiseño	Pala, California
Pauma Reservation	Luiseño	Valley Center, California
Pechanga Reservation	Luiseño	Temecula, California
Ramona Reservation	—	Valle Vista or Anza, California
Resighini Ranchería	Yurok	Klamath, California
Rincon Reservation	Luiseño	Valley Center, California
Roaring Creek Ranchería	Pit River	Montgomery Creek, California
Round Valley Reservation	Mixed (including Wailaki, Yuki, Nomelacki & Pomo)	Covelo, California
Rumsey Ranchería	Wintun	Rumsey, California
San Manuel Reservation	Serrano	San Bernardino, California
San Pasqual Reservation	Luiseño	Valley Center, California
Santa Rosa Ranchería	Tachi	Lemoore, California
Santa Rosa Reservation	Coahuila or Cahuilla	Hemet, California
Santa Ynez Reservation	Chumash	Santa Ynez, California
Santa Ysabel Reservation	Diegueño	Santa Ysabel, California
Sheep Ranch Ranchería	Mewuk	Sheep Ranch, California
Sherwood Valley Ranchería	—	Sherwood Valley Willits, California
Shingle Springs Ranchería	Mewuk	El Dorado, California
Soboba Reservation	Coahuila or Cahuilla	San Jacinto, California
Stewarts Point Ranchería	Kashia Band of Pomo	Stewarts Point, California
Strathmore Ranchería	—	Strathmore, California
Sulphur Bank Ranchería	Pomo	Clearlake Oaks, California
Susanville Ranchería	Paiute & Maidu	Susanville, California
Sycuan Reservation	Diegueño	El Cajon, California
Torres-Martinez	Coahuila or Cahuilla	Thermal, California
Trinidad Ranchería	Yurok	Trinidad, California
Tule River Reservation	Tule River	Porterville, California
Tuolumne Ranchería	Mewuk	Tuolumne, California
Twenty-Nine Palms Reservation	Serrano	Twenty-Nine Palms, California
Yuima Reservation— Part of Pauma Reservation	Luiseño	Valley Center, California
X L Ranch Reservation	Pit River	Alturas, California

ACREAGE OF MAJOR RESERVATIONS

1) FORT YUMA RESERVATION—Winterhaven (southeast area of California) 9141 acres
2) HOOPA VALLEY—Hoopa (northwest area of California) 86277 acres
3) HOOPA VALLEY EXTENSION—Weitchpec 7092 acres
4) PALM SPRINGS (AGUA CALIENTE) RESERVATION—Palm Springs (southern California) 29967 acres
5) TULE RIVER RESERVATION—Porterville (Tulare County) 54116 acres

INDIAN POPULATION

THE 1955 UNITED STATES CENSUS:

39,014 Indians living in California (mostly in Los Angeles, Humboldt, and San Diego counties). Of this number about 7600 live on or near reservations; the balance live in rural areas, towns and cities (mostly in the Los Angeles and San Francisco Bay areas). This total population of the state includes Indians who have come to live in California from other states. (A California Indian is considered to be one who can trace his ancestry back to an Indian living in California on June 1, 1852.) Since the above Census there have been changes but presently there is no other official Indian population count.

TOTAL INDIAN POPULATION IN THE UNITED STATES:

In 1850 — 250,000 Indians

Between 1900–1950 — 400,000 Indians living on or near reservations

By 1970 — 700,000 or more estimated Indian population, a figure that shows that the Indian people do not belong to a vanishing race.

INDIAN SCHOOL POPULATION: (AS OF 1967)

275 Indian schools and dormitories, including high schools
59,000 (approximately) Indian children in Indian schools
100,000 (approximately) Indian children in public schools

INDIAN CALENDAR

Those were the days when time did not stand still but there were no calendars and no clocks. No one knew his exact age. Most groups did not even have a word for "year" but used the word "world" instead. At the end of the cold season, an Indian might have said, "the world went," meaning that the cold time was over.

Probably every group, however, had its own way of telling time during the year. The Maidu knew twelve moons, beginning in the spring season. The Yurok calendar counted moons beginning with the middle of winter. Some could tell the time of the year by the stars. Some put knots in a string to count the days. Nature told the time of the year by when different foods were ready to be gathered. Indians knew exactly which foods ripened in each season. Each month had a certain meaning to these people. A sample of this is found in the Pomo group.

POMO CALENDAR

January	Buckeyes ripen
February	Cold winds blow
March	Growth begins
April	Flowers begin to bloom
May	Seeds ripen
June	Bulbs mature
July	Manzanita ripens
August	Acorns appear
September	Soaproot dug
October	Trees cut down
November	Cold Begins
December	Leaves yellow and fall

SOME OF THE IMPORTANT PLANTS USED FOR MEDICINE*

PLANT	USES
Calabazilla	Pulp of green fruit mixed with soap, put on sores
Camas	Crushed bulbs used for boils, snake bites after poison removed
Creosote Bush	Used for many ailments, used widely
Douglas Fir	Brew from branches for lung trouble
Indian Tobacco	Much used by *shamans*. Cure for earache, toothache, pain, sores
Indigo Bush	Desert tribes' "cure-all" for many ills
Jimson Weed (Tololache)	Bruises, sores, snake bites, etc.
Madrone	Brews from roots, bark; leaves used for colds, headache, skin rash
Manzanita	Tonic from leaves for colds, headache, skin rash, etc.
Mesquite	Sore throat, sore eyes (gum was dissolved in water)
Mexican Tea (Squaw Tea)	Tea made for tonic, kidney ills, colds, stomach, etc.
Milkweed	Gum from boiled juice for sores, warts, ringworm; tea for coughs
Piñon Gum	Hot resin used for sores, cuts, insect bites, body pains
Poison Oak	Juice used for warts, bites, ringworm
Squawbush	Smallpox, sores, skin rash
Tansy Mustard	Stomach ills (especially for children), poultice
Toyon	Tea made for stomach-ache, body pains
Turkey Mullein	Fevers, chills, internal pain, asthma
White Alder	Bitter bark tea used widely for stomach ills, to clear blood, fever
Yerba Mansa	Important "cure-all." Peppery root dried, used for sore throat; powder put on boils, cuts, sores (also used for animal sores)
Yerba Santa	Cure for colds, sore throat, body pains, fever; purify blood

*Plants varied by area and this list includes some of the most important medicinal plants and their uses. Without modern drugs, medical doctors, hospitals and clinics, Indians were able to find and prepare medicines from plants that cured them of many ills. This is another example of how they lived close to nature and made wide use of the plant life that nature offered them. They did much to help early settlers in the way of using plants for healthful purposes. Men are still studying plants and trying to find even more ways in which they can be used for healing.

PLANTS USED IN BASKETMAKING AND FOR DYES*

PLANT	USES
Barberry	Yellow dye for baskets or fabrics
Bear Grass	Fibers split from leaves. Many of central and northern California tribes used them for white overlay in woven baskets, sometimes as patterns
Chain Fern	Red-dyed root fibers used in patterns
Deer Grass	Widely used by southern California Indians for foundation of coiled baskets
Douglas Fir	Smaller roots eight to ten feet long used for basketmaking
Elderberry	Dye from berries and stems
Five-Leaf Fern	Yellow-brownish dye for basket patterns
Indian Hemp	Fiber used for nets, carrying baskets, in making cords and ropes
Poison Oak	Slender stems used in woven baskets. Juice used for black dye in patterns
Squawbush	Silky fiber from leaves made into cords, nets, bags, snares in catching animals
White Alder	Red dye from bark; chewed bark and made red spittle for dye
Woodwardia Fern	Used for very fine baskets, caps for watertight cooking vessels overlaid with beautiful white fibers
Yucca: Our Lord's Candle	Good thread from leaf fibers; pointed end used for needle
Yucca: Spanish Bayonet	Inner part of roots used for red or brown strands in baskets

* Indian women knew exactly where to find the finest materials and dyes to be used in their basketmaking and they spent many hours in gathering the very best plants for this purpose.

OTHER USES FOR PLANTS BY THE INDIANS*

PLANT	USES
Amole (Soap Plant)	Crushed bulb used for soap; when dried, ground into powder (like soap powder) putting feathers on arrow shafts
	Crushed bulb put in streams; fish floated to top and easily caught
	Thick juice of baked bulbs used as glue for putting feathers on arrowshafts
	Juice of leaves used for tattooing
Calabazilla	Root cut into pieces, used like cakes of soap
Douglas Fir	Soot from gum used for tattooing
Indian Tobacco	Leaves used for smoking
Jimson Weed	Drink made to induce dreams in boys' coming-of-age rites
Madrone	Charcoal used in making gunpowder
Mesquite	For chewing gum and glue, blue dye, shampoo
Milkweed	Gum
Saltbush	Roots used as soap
Sea Blite (Glasswort)	Ashes used in making soap
Soap Plant	Crushed roots used for soap. When dried, ground into powder (like soap powder)
Turkey Mullein	For catching fish (as *Amole*)
	Poison for tipping arrows
White Alder	Bark chewed and red spittle used on bodies to lure fish into nets
	For arrow shafts
Yerba Santa	Some used dried leaves as tobacco. Chewed it; quenched thirst on journeys

* In addition to the above varied uses for plants, Indians made pleasant drinks from the Barberry, Lemonade Berry, Sugarbush Berry, and many others.

Chart of Tribes,
Locations, and Main Differences

CHART OF TRIBES, LOCATIONS, AND MAIN DIFFERENCES

TRIBE (Family)	TERRITORY	CLOTHES AND ORNAMENTS	HOUSES
TOLOWA (Athabascan)	Smith River, Del Norte County, close to Oregon.		
HUPA (Athabascan)	Trinity River.		
CHILULA (Athabascan)	Lower Redwood Creek, along redwood belt to a few miles above Minor Creek.		Had plank houses.
WHILKUT (Athabascan)	Redwood Creek above Chilula and Mad River, wedged in between Wiyot and Wintun.		Bark slab houses. The sweat house was earth-covered as in central California.
MATTOLE (Athabascan)	Cape Mendocino by Bear River, Mattole River, and few miles of Eel River.		
NONGATL (Athabascan)	Along Eel River, creeks in area, and upper waters of Mad River.		
SINKYONE (Athabascan)	South Fork—Eel River and coast above Shelter Cove to point between Usal and Rockport, where they met the coast Yuki.	Used yellow-hammer feather headbands as in central California.	Cone-shaped and made of bark slabs.
LASSIK (Athabascan)	Few miles above mouth of South Fork and to head of Mad River.		Same as Sinkyone.
KATO "lake" (Athabascan)	Northernmost courses of South Fork of Eel River.		

This chart indicates some of the main differences among the various Indian tribes. Blank spaces have been left where the things they made and their customs were alike and are described elsewhere in the book.

FOOD	BASKETS	BOATS	CUSTOMS AND OTHER INFORMATION
		Redwood dugout canoes, twice as long as any other tribe had.	Much like Yurok and Hupa.
			Traded with the Yurok. Gave animal skins and inland foods for redwood canoes and seafoods.
		No boats.	Little known about them.
	Very few baskets.		
	Some baskets but not too well made.		Ceremonies few and simple. They were considered a poor tribe.
			Caught deer by driving them into corrals made of logs.
			Redwood country. Nearly fifty villages; some still left at Round Valley Reservation (others near Laytonville). Had customs like Yuki but Kato and Yuki had quarrels. Women smeared black pitch on face if there was a death in the family.

TRIBE (Family)	TERRITORY	CLOTHES AND ORNAMENTS	HOUSES
WAILAKI "north language" (Athabascan)	On Eel River farthest north.		
YUROK (Algonkin)	Along Klamath River.	Haliotis shells on fringes of women's aprons. Wore many ornaments. Women parted hair, bound like clubs, over each shoulder. On special occasions added fur or woodpecker scalps to hair style. Widows cut hair very short.	Redwood plank and the more ridges, the richer the person was supposed to be. Hard earthen floors.
WIYOT (Algonkin)	Lower Mad River, Humboldt Bay, and lower Eel River, mostly redwood forest land. Villages by stream, bay, or tidewater. Ocean front low and sandy.		
HUCHNOM "mountain people" (Yukian)	Redwood valley near one of sources of Russian River, valley of the South Eel.		

FOOD	BASKETS	BOATS	CUSTOMS AND OTHER INFORMATION
Were great hunters. Caught elk and deer by running them down. Also did well in fishing.			More Athabascans here than any other part of the state except Hoopa (Hupa) Valley.
Ate more salmon than others. Better food than many tribes. Had fancy company spoons and many more utensils than others.	Flat basket caps. Conical carrying baskets. Used very large storage baskets. Large flat baskets for deer meat. Large ones for washing hands after feasts.	Dugout redwood log boats. Sold them to Hupa and Karok tribes. Used them mostly on rivers.	Had no chief. Yurok wanted very much to be rich. Were not warlike. If any damage, they paid for it; if anyone killed, family of deceased was paid. Had unusual chisel-like tool, a blade lashed to stone handle. Only Yurok had this kind. Used no rattles in their music or ceremonies. Had no Girls' Ceremony but when five years old, girls were tattooed with a black stripe from corner of mouth to below the chin. Tribe had sharp obsidian arrow points. Men had great speed in running. As they ran they prayed to sun and moon in singsong way. Yurok were outdoor people and loved all of nature.
		Canoes much like Yurok.	*Shaman* were women; received their power on mountaintops at night. They had headbands from which hung two strings of feathers.
			Called the "Redwoods people" by white men. Were friendly with the Pomo; hunted, fished, and traded with them. The Huchnom were very religious like the Yuki. During Boys' Ceremony the Pomo and Kato joined in ceremony with their boys.

165

TRIBE (Family)	TERRITORY	CLOTHES AND ORNAMENTS	HOUSES
COAST YUKI (Yukian)	Along coast between Kato and Pomo territories.		Cone-shaped bark house with steep roof.
YUKI (Yukian)	Along Coast Range Mountains. All land lying in drainage of Eel River above the North Fork except along South Eel River.	Men wore string head nets. Women tattooed chins only.	Cone-shaped and earth-covered. Short, low entrance. Took two days to build; lasted about two years.
WAPPO "brave" (Yukian)	Held territory north of Sonoma Creek; valley of Napa River.		
MODOC (Lutuamian)	Northern border of the state.	Wore tule leggings to the knee. Shredded tule blanket worn by women. Used snow-shoes in winter.	Underground earth-covered brush house. Used steam not fire in sweat house.

166

FOOD	BASKETS	BOATS	CUSTOMS AND OTHER INFORMATION
Salmon swimming upstream speared with two-pronged harpoons. Salmon swimming downstream caught with nets. Caught surf fish in net.	Made string from fibers of iris leaves.		Probably part of Huchnom, not Yuki family. Friendly with all their neighbors even though Yuki warred with the Kato. They wrapped their dead in deerskin or bearskin.
	Coiled baskets woven from right to left, unlike most tribes who wove from left to right. Made some baskets as flat as plates and some tiny ones for gifts or to hold some treasure. No basket caps worn by women.		A short people but had longest heads of any tribe. Had chiefs in large villages only. Yuki rarely went to the coast. War-like and fought all their neighbors at various times. Had many ceremonies. Counted spaces between fingers (4), not fingers (5), and so counted by 8's (spaces between the two hands), not 10's (fingers). Rich man was called a "person man"—a man who was a real person. Chief was rich, friendly, and always ready to help. Richer people paid for a wife; wife's parents made a return in gifts. No mourning ceremony. Usually buried in large baskets along with some of the person's property.
			Language much like Pomo. Many low mountains in their territory but they were a valley people.
No acorns. Ate mostly meat, fish, and water-lily seeds.	Twined, soft baskets of tule with porcupine quills. Put design both outside and inside.	Dugout canoe and tule canoes. Tule ones when hunting and warfare, paddled with their hands.	More war-like than other tribes. Band bound around baby's head to make it high and narrow. Used board cradles for babies.

TRIBE (Family)	TERRITORY	CLOTHES AND ORNAMENTS	HOUSES
ACHOMAWI (Hokan)	Pit River area (a stream people).	Deerskins used. Cut hole in middle, slipped over head. Skin sewed together at side seams.	Bark house, entered from the roof.
ATSUGEWI (Hokan)	Lived on three streams that drained northward into Pit River.		About the same
YANA (Hokan)	Pit River and on edge of Sacramento Valley. Landmark in area was Mt. Lassen.		Earth-covered house.
YAHI (Hokan)	Mill and Deer creeks that run into Sacramento River.		Lived part of the time in caves.
KAROK "upstream" (Hokan)	Three clusters of towns at mouths of Camp Creek, Salmon River, and Clear Creek. Along other parts of river were smaller villages.		
CHIMARIKO (Hokan)	Along twenty-mile stretch of Trinity River from mouth of South Fork to French Creek.		Houses had walls of bark, not planks.
SHASTAN (Hokan)	Klamath River, on Scott River and Shasta River. Limits formed by watershed that separates Sacramento, Trinity, and Salmon River from Mt. Shasta to Oregon mountains.	Made more use of skins because they lived in colder climate. Women wore hair in two wrapped clubs, "Yurok style."	

FOOD	BASKETS	BOATS	CUSTOMS AND OTHER INFORMATION
Not many acorns. Caught deer in deer pits. Pit River got its name from the deer pits in the area.	Twined soft baskets; not too well made.	Dug out pine or cedar.	Few ceremonies. Buried dead in basket in sitting-up position. Widow cut off hair and made belt of it. Today the tribe is one of two most populous Indian communities. (See also *Atsugewi*.)
as the Achomawi.			Lived just south of the Achomawi. Today is one of two most populous Indian communities. (See also *Achomawi*.)
			Best warriors in the area; much feared by their neighbors. Had native dog much like coyote and used it for hunting. Tribe was very plain in its living.
Used manzanita wood for making beautifully carved spoons. Sowed tobacco seeds in forests; only tribe to grow tobacco plants.			They were like their neighbors (Yurok) in almost everything. Never saw a white man until Gold Rush days. Had many ceremonies, at the beginning of each season especially. Had Girls' Ceremony also.
		River too small and rough for canoes, so they waded or swam across streams.	Poorer than the Yurok and Hupa. One of small tribes and miners may have killed most of them.
Mixed dry, powdered berries with meal to sweeten it. Pine nuts steamed, dried, and stored for winter.	Made few and so traded to get them.		Traded with the Kurok. Received dentalium shells, baskets, acorns. Gave deerskins, obsidian. Families made and owned own dams. Chief was head of richest family. No dancing except for war or to give *shaman* power to cure illness.

TRIBE (Family)	TERRITORY	CLOTHES AND ORNAMENTS	HOUSES
YUMA (Hokan)	Mostly the western bank of Colorado River and to mouth of Gila River.		
WASHO (Hokan)	Upper drainage of Truckee and Carson rivers. Lake Tahoe in center of their territory.		Dome-shaped houses, thatched with tule, leaves, or bark.
ESSELEN (Hokan)	Near part of Carmel River and rocky coast for twenty-five miles from near Point Sur to Point López.		
SALINAN (Hokan)	Near Santa Margarita Divide, north to Santa Lucia Peak, and somewhere south of Soledad.		
CHUMASH (Hokan)	Along Pacific Coast from Malibu Canyon to Point Concepción and northward to Estero Bay.		Records show that some of their houses were very large—for as many as fifty people. Used mat curtains between rooms. Had raised beds.

FOOD	BASKETS	BOATS	CUSTOMS AND OTHER INFORMATION
			Mourning ceremony for chiefs only. Both the Yuma and Mohave were war-like. Unlike any other tribes they used a shield when at war. Unlike all other California tribes, Yuma tribe learned how to farm and irrigate crops. Today Fort Yuma has about 900 residents.
	Coiled baskets. Noted for excellent finish and design.		They were known as "Basin People."
			Smallest of all tribes and first to disappear. Probably lived in other places in the beginning and were pushed into a corner. Very little known about them.
			Traded and visited freely with the Yokuts. The Costonoans to the north were their enemies.
	Baskets sealed with asphalt. Used for holding water. Were very well made.	Had finest boats in California or any other place in the United States at that time. Their next-door neighbors, the Salinans, had none.	Had many large villages. Had charmstones that were highly prized. Once they were a very important group. Went to sea more than any other tribe. Had spears for catching sea otters and seals.

TRIBE (Family)	TERRITORY	CLOTHES AND ORNAMENTS	HOUSES
POMO (Hokan)	Valley of the Russian River and all canyons of Coast Ranges. Its territory was coast, Russian River Valley, and Clear Lake district.	Skirts were of inner redwood bark fibers and tule grass. Sandals and leggings of tule; some of netted string. Men wore ear tubes made of bird bones or wooden rods tipped with feathers.	Homes along lakes in summer and along streams in winter. Loved to live in sunny places. Houses were redwood bark and cone-shaped, thatched with bundles of grass.
DIEGUEÑO "southerners" (Hokan)	Bordered by the Pacific Ocean and on the west by the Luiseño, Cupeño, and Cahuilla on the north (San Diego area). It is believed that the Kamia lived in the Imperial Valley but little is known about this.		House earth-covered. Three posts in row, log across top, poles leaned from the side. Covered with brush, then earth. Tent-shaped, unlike most other tribes.

FOOD	BASKETS	BOATS	CUSTOMS AND OTHER INFORMATION
Ocean gave them mussels, surf fish, and sea lions. In winter the salmon ran upstream in rivers and creeks and was plentiful. Small game all year. Everywhere in their area there was plenty of food of all kinds.	No basket caps; used broad band on head. Their twined baskets called the finest baskets made in the world. Their coiled baskets used for gifts and trading. Made great use of tiny bright feathers and beads. Most tribes made about thirty wrappings an inch; the Pomo made sixty or more. Made sitting-up cradles.	Tule rush canoes on lakes. Coast people used redwood logs along shore but had no real boats.	One of best-known groups in California. Many villages—seventy-five large ones and almost five hundred smaller ones. Chief lived in largest village. Pomo owned salt beds and traded salt for goods from other tribes. Some of Pomo tribe still left. Had large earth-covered "dancing houses." Pomo were bankers of central California and made lots of shell money. Their tubular beads of magnesite were most prized, called "their gold." Had two kinds of chiefs: Great and Lesser.
	Made some pottery. In addition to baskets they made close-twined sacks or wallets of milkweed fiber. String colored red or white. Burden nets made of yucca fiber.		Not friendly to those at Mission San Diego; attacked, burned, and killed mission priest, the only priest who met death at hand of Indians in the history of the missions. They still occupy trust lands in the mission area.

TRIBE (Family)	TERRITORY	CLOTHES AND ORNAMENTS	HOUSES
MOHAVE (Hokan)	Southeast corner of state, on Colorado River.	Believed in tattooing and painting of faces more than other groups. Shells used more as ornaments than money. Loved all kinds of beads. Would trade almost anything to get beads.	Frame of poles, thatched and covered with sand. Men put up large sleeping houses for themselves.
WINTUN (Penutian)	West side of Sacramento Valley from Sacramento River up to crest of Coast Range, Suisun, and San Pablo Bay, Napa, and perhaps part of Sonoma Valley.		
MAIDU (Penutian)	Feather and American rivers from Sacramento River east to crest of Sierra Nevada Mountains.		Bed was raised from floor. Pine needles used to make it soft. Many water birds in area and so blankets made of feathers.

FOOD	BASKETS	BOATS	CUSTOMS AND OTHER INFORMATION
Planted beans, wheat, pumpkins, water-melons, cantaloupes.	Made coiled pottery but very poor baskets.		Fought tribes hun-dreds of miles away (as far as Chumash and Yokuts terri-tories). Were friends with the Chemeheuvi because they let them pass through their area on way to trade or make war against other tribes. Used heavy clubs more than bows and arrows. The Mohave were tall, large-boned, and thin. Had a yellowish skin color and tied up their hair with clay. They laughed freely and were not shy. They thought that every dream would come true. They had few ceremonies. Normal pace when traveling was a trot. Today Fort Mohave Reserva-tion has less than three hundred resi-dents.
			Largest group in northern half of California. Had many kinds of dances (most important was Ghost Dance). Had men's secret society, the Kuksu.
Salmon, eels, eggs of yellow jackets, in-sects, grasshoppers were eaten.	Coiled baskets. Used willow and unpeeled redbud. Twined bas-kets for traps.	Used log rafts and flat dugout canoes and also tule. Usually tribes had one or the other; Maidu had both.	They counted shell money by 10's, not by length of string. For fishing, had net on end of pole. Also had secret Kuksu society. *Hesi* was chief dance—October and May.

TRIBE (Family)	TERRITORY	CLOTHES AND ORNAMENTS	HOUSES
YOKUTS (Penutian)	Whole San Joaquin Valley from mouth of San Joaquin River to foot of Tehachapi Pass; lower hills of Sierra Nevada from Fresno River south.	Women wore headband with upright feather in the back.	Had several kinds of houses: cone-shaped, round, oblong. The oblong had shade porch in front.
MIWOK (Penutian)	Long slope of Sierra Nevada Mountains looking out over the San Joaquin Valley, Marin County, and part of Sonoma Valley. Were Coast, Lake, and Plains Miwok.		
COSTONOANS "coast people" (Penutian)	San Francisco Bay area, south to Point Sur, on east to Mt. Diablo.	Wore rabbit-skin coat during day, and used it as blanket at night. Men put mud on bodies in cold mornings until sun warmed them.	
PAIUTE-NORTHERN (Shoshonean)	Northeast corner of the state.		
MONO "persons" (Shoshonean)	Partly in Great Basin, some in Sierra Nevada Mountains. Eastern Mono lived along base of the mountains. Owens River flowed through territory.		

FOOD	BASKETS	BOATS	CUSTOMS AND OTHER INFORMATION
	Special jar-like baskets. Quail feathers woven in along upper edge. They were called "Tulare bottle-necks." Some of hill tribes made crude pottery by pressing hole in lump of clay.		
	Feather-decorated baskets like the Pomo. Very high storage baskets. Branches around sides. Branches pulled aside and acorns rolled out.		Coast Miwok was tribe that met Sir Francis Drake. He spent five days repairing the *Golden Hind* in Bay now known as Drake's Bay. Indians here believed that white men were spirits returned from the dead and so welcomed them. Also had secret Kuksu society.
Mussels must have been the main food because so many shellmounds found in the area.		Tule rafts used to cross San Francisco Bay.	Ocean front and bay land lined with shell deposits, second only to the Santa Barbara Islands. Painted bodies red and wore feathers more than most tribes.
			Many lakes, swamps, salt basins. Not much is known about them. Not much like any other tribe in the state.
			Still has burning ceremony after one year of mourning. Ceremony lasts all night with dances, chants, and burning of baskets and other articles as tribute to the dead.

TRIBE (Family)	TERRITORY	CLOTHES AND ORNAMENTS	HOUSES
KAWAIISU (Shoshonean)	Home was once in the Tehachapi Mountains. Pressed in by neighbors on all sides.		
SHOSHONEAN— WESTERN (once called Panamint or Koso) (Shoshonean)	Base of Sierra Nevada, through much of desert part of California.		
CHEMEHUEVI (or SOUTHERN PAIUTE) (Shoshonean)	Mountain range south of Death Valley and stretching to about Riverside and Imperial counties. Next to Kawaiisu tribe.		Simple overhead shelters for sun or rain.
TUBATULABAL (Shoshonean)	Area drained by the Kern River down as far as a point halfway between the forks of the river and Bakersfield.		
SERRANO (Shoshonean)	Along San Bernardino mountain range and San Gabriel Mountains west to Mt. San Antonio. San Bernardino County, not quite to city of Riverside.		
GABRIELINO (Shoshonean)	Fertile lands of Los Angeles County, some of Sierra Madre range, half of Orange County, and two islands, Santa Catalina and San Clemente.		

FOOD	BASKETS	BOATS	CUSTOMS AND OTHER INFORMATION
			Little known about them.
Had few acorns but pine nuts were important as were seeds. Used lots of mesquite beans and reed stalks. Tree yucca buds were roasted. Agave was roasted in the ground. Cactus used. Mountain sheep was their meat.			
	Made a few simple pottery articles and painted designs on them. Made excellent baskets.		Chemehuevi is largest territory (but thinly populated) occupied by people having one dialect.
			Used to visit the Yokuts; married some of them. Young eagles were caught, cared for, and set free after taking feathers. Birds, geese, and even young coyotes kept as pets.
			Included the Alliklik, Vanyume. All this Serrano group were known as "mountaineers." Still occupy trust lands in the mission area.
			Richest Indians in the state at time of the missions. Named after Mission San Gabriel. Fernandeño of the same group named after Mission San Fernando. They liked thick shells for money. Had a war club that was a straight heavy stick. Used only *metates* for pounding. Yang-na lived in what is now the Los Angeles city area.

TRIBE (Family)	TERRITORY	CLOTHES AND ORNAMENTS	HOUSES
CUPEÑO (Shoshonean)	Near hot springs of present-day Warner's Ranch.		
JUANEÑO (Shoshonean)	Area in between the Gabrielino and Luiseño.		
LUISEÑO (Shoshonean)	West of the divide that is south of Mt. San Jacinto.	Back skirt that women wore was made of soft inner bark of willow or cottonwood tree. Front skirt made of fiber strings. Tattooing done with juice of berries.	Earth-covered planks, unlike their neighbors.

FOOD	BASKETS	BOATS	CUSTOMS AND OTHER INFORMATION
			Very small group. Later went to Pala.
			Named after Mission San Juan Capistrano. All ceremonies held outdoors. Ceremonies held in atmosphere of great respect. Audience could only whisper. No hunter could eat his own fish or game. Two went together so they could exchange.
Used more seeds of all kinds than acorns. Not many roots eaten. Rats, snakes, squirrels eaten. Rabbits cooked in earth oven or over open fire.	Made clay pots by coiling. Women made fans or seed-beaters from squawbush twigs.	Had pine dugout canoes.	Outdoor ceremonial grounds. Had two entrances—one for dancers, one for others. Rest could look in from outside. Did not believe in sacred animals but in a God who helped them daily. Had a fire dance and stamped out fire with feet. Thought that all dead became stars and so named the stars. Named after Mission San Luis Rey.

TRIBE (Family)	TERRITORY	CLOTHES AND ORNAMENTS	HOUSES
CAHUILLA (Shoshonean) "masters" or "strong ones"	Inland basin between San Bernardino Range and one southward from Mt. San Jacinto. Palm Springs area. The desert Cahuilla were near the Salton Sea.		Early houses were circular; later ones were square or oblong with mat roofs and walls plastered with mud. Had large ceremonial houses. The *ramada* (Spanish word) or shade arbor was also used.

FOOD	BASKETS	BOATS	CUSTOMS AND OTHER INFORMATION
In addition to other food, cactus was used. Fruits and fleshy leaves eaten. They used over sixty varieties of plants. Their seed-beaters were more important than a digging stick.	Made clay-coiled pots; probably learned from Colorado River Indians. Their baskets were very well made and women wove rugs and horse blankets, something not done by any other tribe.		One of most important tribes today in California. The government has brought water to area. Indians' rights are protected. Some (Aqua Calientes band) have land that is now very valuable (Palm Springs). Once there were important trade routes through the Cahuilla territory. Later the routes used by Spanish, Mexican, and American explorers. Today there is fine Indian Museum (Malki) on Morongo Reservation near city of Banning. Celebration on May 30 each year (Ka-wita).

PRONUNCIATION GUIDE

Consonants are pronounced somewhat as in English. The vowels are pronounced as follows:

a as in father (ah)
e as in they (ā)
i as in marine (ē)
o as in note (ō)
u as in flute (oo)
ai as in fire (ī)
au as in now (au)

adobe	ah-doh'-bay	unburned brick dried in the sun
agave	ah-gah'-vay	plant used for food
asphalt	as'-fawlt	black, tar-like substance
atole	ah-toh'-lay	soup-like food made from ground leached acorns
Bahia de los Fumos	Bah-hee'-ah deh lohs Foo'-mohs	Bay of Smokes (near present-day Ventura)
balsa	bahl'-sah	boat made of tule reeds
Cabrillo, Juan Rodríguez	Cahb-reel'-yo, Hwahn Rohd-ree'-gays	Portuguese explorer
cactus	kak'-tus	thorny plant used for food
Carpinteria	Car-peen-ter-ee'-ah	city in Santa Barbara County; means "carpenter shop"
chia	chee'-ah	a kind of sage
Colorado	Koh-loh-rah'-doh	Indians lived near the Colorado River. Means "red" in Spanish
Concepción (Point)	Kohn-sep-see-ohn'	point on California coast
corral	koh-rahl'	pen for animals
coyote	ki-oh'-tee	wild animal
dentalium	den-tay'-lee-uhm	a tooth-like shell used for Indian money
Diomedes	Di-oh-mee'-dees	islands in the Bering Strait
Ferrelo, Bartoloméo	Fay-ray'-lo, Bahr-toh-lo-may'-oh	Spanish explorer
Goleta	Goh-lay'-tah	city in California; means "schooner"
islay (or yslay)	ees'-lay	Indian name for wild plums
Junípero Serra	Hoo-nee'-pay-roh Say'-rah	founder of the first nine missions in California
La Victoria	Lah Veec-toh'-ree-ah	one of Cabrillo's ships
magnesite	mag'-nee-site	a mineral
mano	mah'-no	stone used in grinding on a stone slab (metate)
manzanita	mahn-zhan-nee'-tah	a shrub
mesquite	mehs-keet'	plant with bean-like pods
metate	may-tah'-tay	stone slab used in grinding

moccasin	moc'-kah-zhin or moc'-ah-sin	shoe made of leather
Monterey	Mohn-tay-ray'	city in California
mortar	mohr'-tar	bowl used in pounding
obsidian	ob-seh'-dee-ahn	a volcanic glass
olivella	ohl-ee-veh'-lah	shell used for beads by the Indians
padre	pah'-dray	priest or friar
pestle	pes'-ehl	used to pound acorns and seeds in a mortar
piñole	peen-yo'-lay	flour made from seeds
piñon	peen-yon	pine nuts
Portolá, Gaspar de	Por-toh-lah', Gahs'-pahr day	led first party of soldiers into California
presidio	pray-see'-dee-oh	fort, place where the soldiers lived
pueblo	pway'-blow	town or village
ranchería	rahn-chay-ree'-ah	name given to Indian village
ranchero	rahn-chay'-ro	owner of a ranch
rancho	rahn'-cho	land granted by the Spanish and Mexican governments
Sacramento	Sah-krah-mehn'-toh	capital of California, means sacrament
San Antonio (Mount)	Sahn Ahn-toh'-nee-oh	mountain peak
San Diego	Sahn Dee-ay'-go	city in California
San Fernando	Sahn Fer-nahn'-do	city in California
San Francisco	Sahn Frahn-sees'-co	city in California
San Gabriel	Sahn Gahb'-ree-ehl	city in California
San Gorgonio (Mount)	Sahn Gor-gohn'-ee-oh	mountain peak
San Joaquin	Sahn Ho-ah-keen'	valley in California
San Juan Capistrano	Sahn Hwahn Kah-pees-trahn'-o	city in California
San Luis Obispo	Sahn Lwees Oh-bees'-po	city in California
San Miguel (Island)	Sahn Mee-goo-ehl'	one of the Santa Barbara Channel Islands
San Pedro	Sahn Pay'-droh	city in California
San Salvador	Sahn Sahl'-vah-door	one of Cabrillo's ships
Santa Barbara	Sahn'-tah Bahr'-Bahr-ah	city in California
Santa Catalina (Island)	Sahn'-tah Kah-tah-leen'-ah	island
Santa Rosa	Sahn'-tah Roh'-sah	city in California
shaman	shah'-man	medicine man (or woman)
Shasta (Mount)	Shas'tah	California mountain peak
Sierra Nevada	See-ehr'-rah Nay-vah'-dah	mountain range
steatite	stee'-ah-tite	soapstone used by Indians for bowls, charmstones, etc.
temescal	tay-mehs'-cahl	sweat house
tololache	toh-loh-lah'-chee	Jimson weed used in boys' growing-up ceremony
tomolo	toh'-moh-loh	plank canoe
toyon	toh'-yohn	shrub with red berries (Christmas berries)
tule	too'-lay	reed found in marshy land
Ventura	Vehn-too'-rah	city in California
yucca	yuc'-ah	plant used as a food

Index